BOX
MADE EASY

Backup and Sharing in the Cloud

By James Bernstein

Bernstein, James
Box Made Easy
Part of the Productivity Apps Made Easy series

For more information on reproducing sections of this book or sales of this book,
go to **www.madeeasybookseries.com**

Contents

Introduction

With everything being done online these days, it seems as though you need to know how to master a multitude of technologies just to get your work done. We are expected to know how to use email, texting, social media, cloud-based office productivity services, smartphone apps and so on.

Not too long ago (depending on who you ask), when we wanted to share files and collaborate with our peers, we would have to send files back and forth via email and hope that we were working on the latest version of the file. Doing this would also get complicated when we had many people we were working with on a project at the same time.

Another option was to use what is known as an FTP (File Transfer Protocol) sites to store and share files. But this takes some technical skills to set up, and you also need your own server to store these files on. These are still in use today by businesses but are not practical for the home or small business user.

Fortunately, today we have many options as to where we can store and share our files and it seems like we are almost getting pressured into using these services. For example, when you get a new computer running Windows, it will try and force you to use their online storage platform called OneDrive. And if you have a Google\Gmail account, you automatically get access to their Google Drive service whether you plan on using it or not!

The goal of this book is to get you signed up with Box and comfortable with the interface when it comes to uploading and downloading files and folders. I will also be going over how to share and collaborate with other Box and non-Box users.

Once you understand the main concept of how Box and other cloud storage services work, it will make the experience that much easier and also prepare you to use other online storage services at the same time since not everyone uses Box for their cloud storage needs. So on that note, let's head to the cloud!

Chapter 1 – What is Box?

Before showing you how to use Box, I would like to spend a little time going over what exactly it is and what you will expect to see when you first start using it. I will be working with the free account as well as the Starer account so you can see what you can and can't do with the free account type. I will also be going over some features of the business account so you can see what you get when you break out your wallet!

Cloud Storage Overview
In order to get an understanding of what exactly Box does, you should first have an idea of the concept of cloud storage. You are probably used to storing your files and folders on your hard drive and maybe use a removable USB hard drive or flash drive to back up your files or transfer them between computers.

Doing things this way is fine for many people but if you are going to be sharing your files with others or want a way to backup important files offsite, then using cloud storage might be the solution you need.

The term cloud storage refers to storing your files on servers that are located at other locations around the country, or even around the world. Then when you access your files and folders, you do so via a web browser or client software over the internet. This allows you to work on your files remotely or download them to your local computer and then sync them back with the server when you save them again.

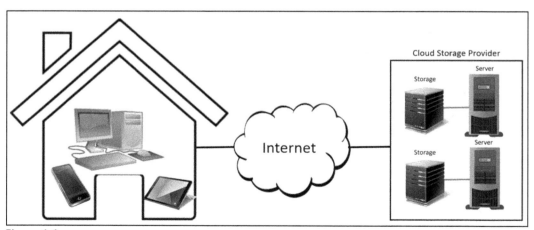

Figure 1.1

Types of Cloud Storage
There are four main types of cloud storage typically in use today. I will be focusing on just one of them, but I wanted to go over the others, so you have an idea of what is available out there.

- **Personal Cloud Storage** – This is what we will be focusing on for the most part and is mainly used to store a user's personal data online, allowing them to access it from anywhere that they have an Internet connection and a device capable of accessing their data. This can be done via a desktop computer, laptop, smartphone, or tablet, and all you need to do is sign into your account and you are off and running.

- **Public Cloud Storage** – This is used when a company doesn't have its own cloud storage resources and all the infrastructure for the storage is managed off-site by another company which also takes care of all aspects of the cloud storage, including making sure it's available all the time and also backed up. Public Cloud Storage providers will store data from many customers all at the same location.

- **Private Cloud Storage** — If a company wants to utilize cloud storage and have it located within their own datacenter but still be managed by a third party, then they can take the private route. This is common when the data is private or confidential and the company needs to know where it is at all times.

- **Hybrid Cloud Storage** — Hybrid Cloud Storage is a combination of Public and Private Cloud Storage where a company will have its critical data stored at its own location while having less important data stored at the cloud provider's location.

Benefits of Cloud Storage
Not all cloud storage is the same, so the benefits will vary based on the type you choose. Since we are only dealing with the personal type, that is what I will be focusing on going forward.

I have many clients that I do work for, and one thing that is very common among a lot of them is the lack of backups. (That is until I force them to start doing them!) If you are like most people, then you have many (or even too many) pictures on your computer as well as music and documents that you would be very upset about losing. If you don't do a backup, then you risk a disaster if your hard drive fails or at least have the potential to spend a lot of money on a data recovery service.

Even if you do backup your data at home or at the office, there's a chance of losing it in situations involving such things as fires or floods. In fact, many companies who do their own local backups will have a service that comes by and takes their backups to a secure location offsite to ensure that they will always be safe.

For us home users having a personal backup assistant is not an option, so we are on our own to make sure we have our data securely backed up. This is where having a cloud storage account can come in handy. If you copy your important files to a location in the cloud, then they are safe there in case something happens to your computer or the location of where your computer is stored. In a worst-case scenario you can get your computer back up and running and then restore your files from your cloud backup right to your computer.

Another benefit of cloud storage is having your data available all the time, no matter where you are. Let's say you are out of town on vacation and brought your laptop or tablet with you and need to get a copy of your resume to apply for a job you want to get in on right away. If you have your data in the cloud, all you would have to do is log on to your account, download your resume, and send it off. Many times, there are options to create a link right to a specific file that you can email to someone, but I will get into that later.

Another way to use cloud storage to your benefit is when you are collaborating with other people on a team project and need to share information. Depending on what cloud provider you go with, you will usually have the option to share files and folders with other people and assign levels of permissions to those people so nobody can get away with doing something they shouldn't be doing to your files, plus it will usually show the last person who made a change to a file with the date and time.

We are all familiar with computer viruses and spyware and how they can ruin our day when they infect our computers. Some of them can even encrypt your files making them inaccessible to you forever. Plus, there's always the chance of you sending an infected file to someone else and infecting their computer. If you have a backup of your files in the cloud, then they will be safe from getting infected (assuming you have not uploaded the infected files to your cloud location).

Disadvantages of Cloud Storage
Many companies use cloud-based storage and applications to save money because they don't need to buy the hardware to support them and hire IT people to maintain them. The main downside is that if you lose your Internet connection

then you lose access to your storage and programs, but for big corporations, it's rare that they have much or any downtime.

For us home users, we have the same types of choices, but on a smaller scale. Here are some of the *disadvantages* of cloud storage:

- **Dependency on the Internet** – Since you need Internet access to get to your files in the cloud, you will have to rely on your Internet service to be up. If you lose your Internet connection, then you won't be able to access your files unless you downloaded a copy to your computer. Home users tend to not have the same reliability when it comes to their Internet connection as big companies do. That's most likely because these corporate accounts cost much more money.

- **Trusting a third party with your data** – Since you don't know *exactly* where your files are being stored and who *really* has access to them, you will have to put some trust in your cloud provider. For all you know, your files may be sitting somewhere in another country with who knows who looking at them.

- **Cost** – Many cloud storage providers will allow you to have a small amount of storage space for free with the plan of enticing you to buy more space once you fill up the free space they've provided. This can get costly if you have a lot of data since the free accounts will only hold so much.

- **Performance** – If you have a slow Internet connection or have huge files, then you will need to wait for your files to download or upload. Plus, if you are working on your smartphone using your cellular connection, it might be even slower.

For the most part, you have nothing to lose in trying out a free cloud storage provider like Box, OneDrive or Dropbox to see if it is something you would like to use on a regular basis. Then you can determine if the cost is worth the advantages you get from keeping your data in the cloud, or if you don't feel comfortable using this type of service.

Box Plans and Pricing
Just like with most online services, Box offers a free plan as well as many subscription-based plans. These plans are broken down into individual and team plans and then business plans.

As of this writing, there are three available plans for individual and team accounts as shown in figure 1.2. As you can see, only one of them is free and with this account you get 10 GB (gigabytes) of storage space and a 250 MB (megabyte) file upload limit meaning you can upload a file as large as 250 MB at one time. One reason to use one of the subscription plans is to increase the file version limit past only one version. I will be discussing file versions later in the book.

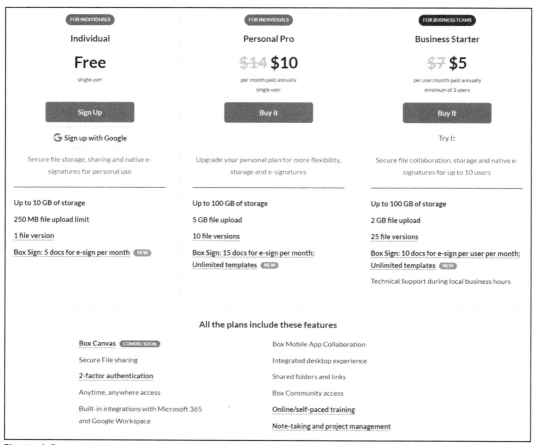

Figure 1.2

At the bottom of figure 1.2, you can see the additional features you get with either of these plans. Figure 1.3 shows the business plans and as you can see, they contain a lot of features but will also cost you a bit more money since the price is per user and you need a minimum of three users for these types of plans.

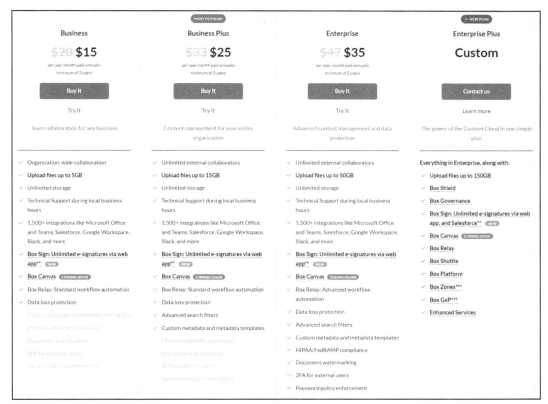

Figure 1.3

Signing Up for an Account

In order to start using Box, you will need to create a username and password that you will use to log into your account. When you go to the Box website, there will be a *Sign Up* button under each of the account types so you will simply click the button under the account type you wish to use.

You will notice that for the free account, you can sign up using your Google account which means you will tie your Google account to your Box account and use the same login for both. I prefer to set up an individual account so my Google account is not tied to a bunch of third party apps.

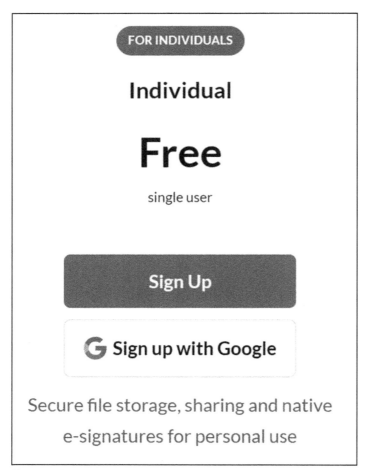

Figure 1.4

If you choose the individual account type, your username will be the email address used to sign up for the account and then you will need to come up with a secure password to go along with it. If you want to read the terms of service or privacy policy before signing up, you can do so at the bottom of the page. When you are ready to create your account, simply click on the *Get Started* button to have it created.

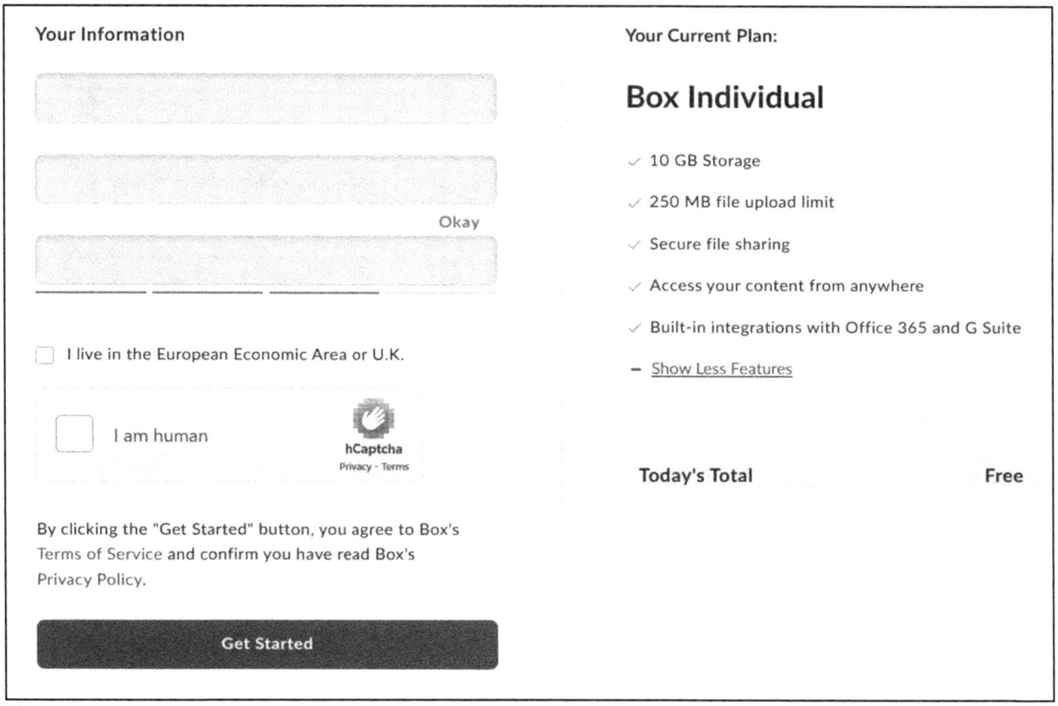

Your Information

Your Current Plan:

Box Individual

✓ 10 GB Storage

Okay

✓ 250 MB file upload limit

✓ Secure file sharing

✓ Access your content from anywhere

✓ Built-in integrations with Office 365 and G Suite

☐ I live in the European Economic Area or U.K.

— Show Less Features

☐ I am human

hCaptcha
Privacy - Terms

Today's Total   **Free**

By clicking the "Get Started" button, you agree to Box's Terms of Service and confirm you have read Box's Privacy Policy.

Get Started

Figure 1.5

You will then get an email with a link that you will need to click on to confirm your email address and then you will be all ready to go.

The Box Interface

The first time you sign into your Box account, don't expect to see too much since you will not have any files or folders there since it's a new account. Figure 1.6 shows the initial welcome screen with the *Get Started* button at the bottom of the page.

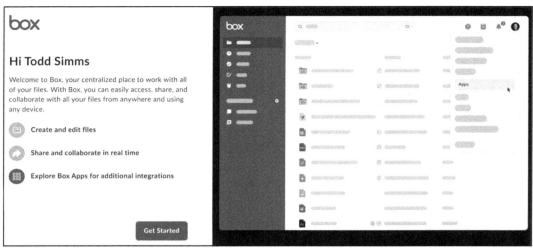

Figure 1.6

Once you get into the actual Box interface, you will see all of the navigation items on the left where you will be spending a lot of your time. Then in the main part of the screen you will have all of your files and folders. Since this is a new account, I only have the *Getting Started with Box* PDF file that comes with my account. I can either keep this file to read about Box or delete it if I do not need it.

Figure 1.7

At the top of the file list, you will have the default columns such as the names of the files and folders, updated date and owner name, and their size. To the right of the size column, there is an icon with four boxes that will change your file view from a list style to a grid style. Then the arrow next to that is used to hide the sidebar if you need more space on the screen.

The sidebar is used to see details about a file or folder. When you check the selection box next to a file, you will be shown a preview of the file if it's a supported file type as well as information about that file (or folder).

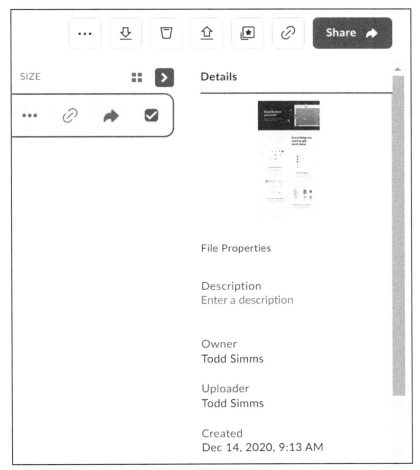

Figure 1.8

Another thing you will notice in figure 1.8 is that when you select a file or folder, you get some additional icons\buttons at the top of the screen. These are used for tasks such as moving, copying, deleting, sharing, downloading and so on. I will get into these tasks in greater detail as we go along.

At the upper right of the Box interface, you will see a button that says *New* (figure 1.9). This is where you will click to do things such as upload files and folders and create a variety of document types such as Word documents, Google Docs, spreadsheets, Box notes etc.

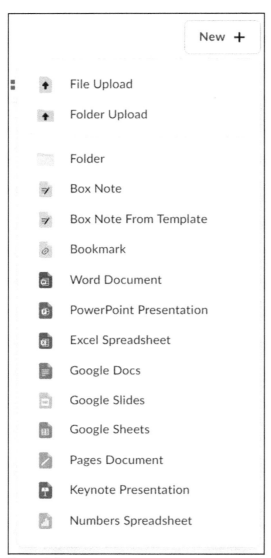

Figure 1.9

At the lower left corner of the screen, you will see an indicator bar showing how much of your total available space you have used.

Figure 1.10

Chapter 2 – Adding Files and Folders

Now that you have a better understanding of how the Box interface looks and functions, it's time to start uploading and creating some files so we can get our data backed up and share files with colleagues later.

Uploading Files and Folders

There are a couple of ways to go about uploading files and folders to your Box online storage. One way is to click on the *New* button at the upper right and then choose either *File Upload* or *Folder Upload*.

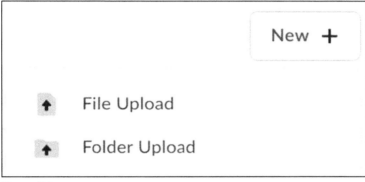

Figure 2.1

Whether you are choosing to upload a file or a folder, you will need to browse your computer to find the one you are looking for. I want to upload some Hawaii photos from my computer and will upload the entire Hawaii folder rather than create a folder manually and then upload the individual files. Once I locate the folder on my computer, I can click the *Upload* button to start the process.

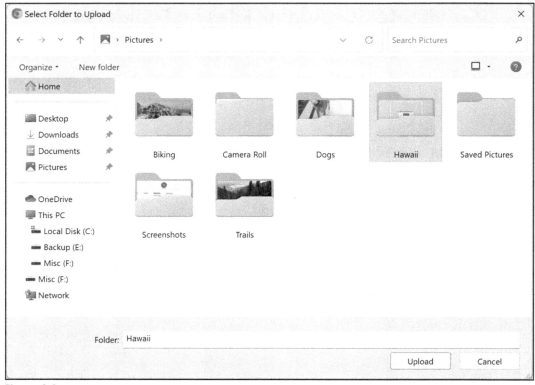

Figure 2.2

I will then be shown a notification asking me to confirm that I wish to upload the folder and its associated files.

Figure 2.3

Now I can see my newly uploaded folder in my *All Files* section and it shows that there are 16 files within this folder.

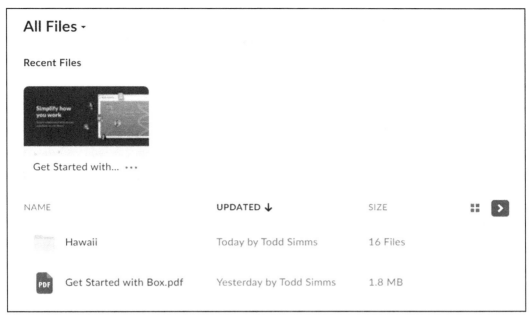

Figure 2.4

Now I will upload some individual files to my main Box area, as in they will not be in a folder. This time I will click the New button and choose *File Upload* and select just the files I want to upload. This time you will notice that you need to click on *Open* rather than Upload.

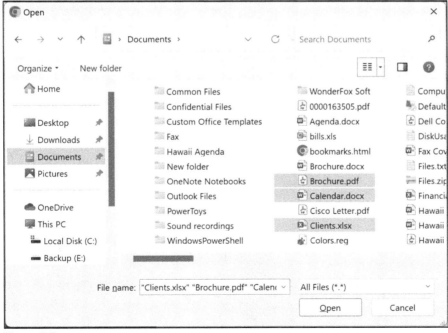

Figure 2.5

Now you can see that I have my new files uploaded in my All Files section along with my Hawaii folder and the Get Started with Box PDF file that was already in my account when I logged in for the first time.

All Files ‑	
NAME	UPDATED ↓
📁 Hawaii	Today by Todd Simms
📄 Calendar.docx	Today by Todd Simms
📄 Brochure.pdf	Today by Todd Simms
📊 Clients.xlsx	Today by Todd Simms
📄 Get Started with Box.pdf	Yesterday by Todd Simms

Figure 2.6

Another method for uploading files and folders is to drag and drop them from your computer into the Box website itself. The process works the same whether you are uploading files or folders. As you can see in figure 2.7, all I need to do is select the files or folders on my computer and drag them into the Box website and they will be uploaded for me.

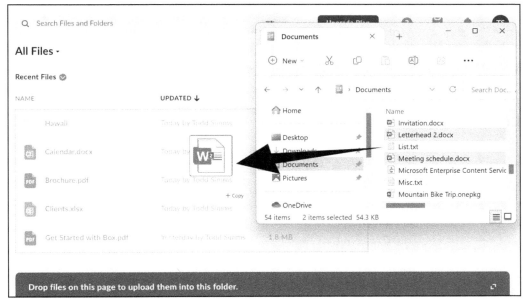

Figure 2.7

If I wanted to drag some files into a folder that I have in my Box account, I would need to open that folder within Box first and then drag the files into the Box web page. The same goes for uploading using the New button method.

Creating Files and Folders

If you are planning on creating your files or folders on the Box website rather than uploading them from your computer, it is a similar process to accomplish this. To create a folder, you would simply click the New button and then click on *Folder* rather than *Folder Upload*.

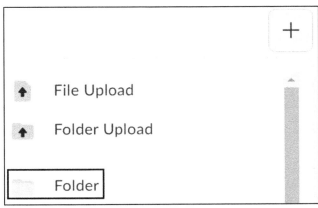

Figure 2.8

You will then be asked to give the folder a name and can optionally invite people to access this new folder as well as change the share permission to that folder. Since I will not be setting up any shared folders yet, I will just type in *Sales Files* for the folder name and leave the rest blank and click the *Create* button.

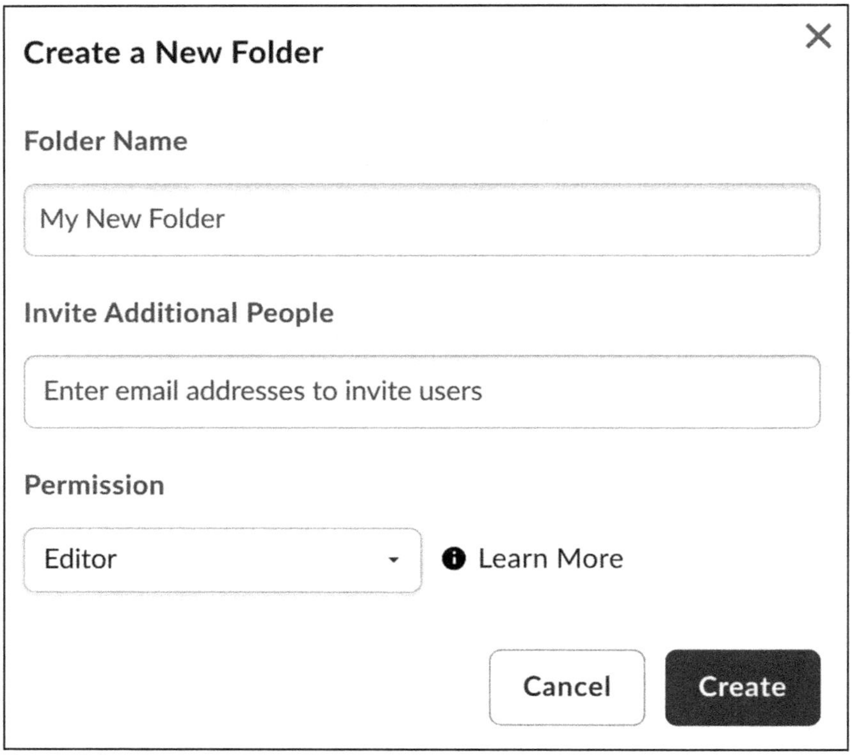

Create a New Folder   ×

Folder Name

My New Folder

Invite Additional People

Enter email addresses to invite users

Permission

Editor   ▾   ⓘ Learn More

Cancel   **Create**

Figure 2.9

My new folder will then show up in the location I was in when I clicked on the New button to create it.

The process for creating files varies quite a bit from creating folders because a folder is a folder but there are many different types of files that you can create. As you saw in the last chapter, when you click on the New button, there are many file types to choose from as seen in figure 2.10.

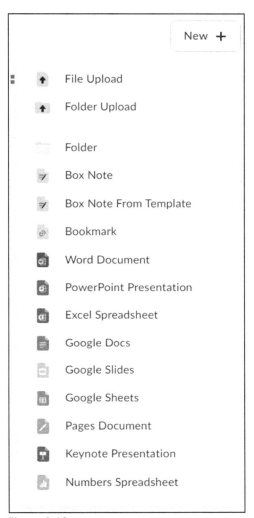

Figure 2.10

Many of these file types should be recognizable to you such as Word Documents, Excel Spreadsheets and Google Docs. Word, PowerPoint and Excel are all Microsoft products that you can access online via an Office 365 account or the free Office Online apps. Google Docs, Slides and Sheets are all part of the free Google Apps that you can use online. Pages, Keynote and Numbers are online Apple apps. I will be going over Box Notes later in this book which is owned by Box itself.

If I were to choose a new *Google Docs* file, I would then be prompted to enter a name for my new document. I will call this new file *Holiday Schedule* and then click the *Create* button.

Create a Google Doc   ✕

Name

|

Cancel   Create

Figure 2.11

The first time you create a Google file, you might be prompted to accept the Google Workspace agreement before being able to continue. You might also run into this for the Microsoft and Apple apps.

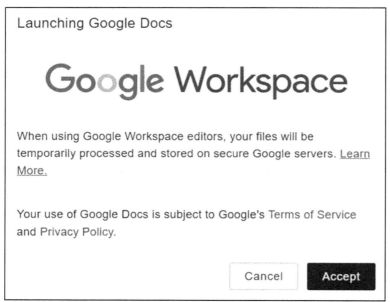

Figure 2.12

You will then be taken to your open Google Doc file where you can begin editing it as needed. When I go back to my Box file listing, I will now see my new Holiday Schedule document there. If you are wondering what the V2 next to the name indicates, that is for file versioning which I will be discussing later in the book.

All Files ·

Recent Files ✅

NAME	UPDATED ↓	SIZE
Sales Files	Today by Todd Simms	0 Files
Hawaii	Today by Todd Simms	17 Files
Holiday Schedule.gdoc V2 ⚇	Today by Todd Simms	8.3 KB
Meeting schedule.docx	Today by Todd Simms	11.7 KB

Figure 2.13

Bookmarks

Box has a nice feature that will allow you to save website links to your Box account and then share them with others if needed. This way you have easy access to saved websites right from the same area you access your files, so you won't have to leave the Box interface to access those websites.

To create a bookmark, simply click on the New button and then choose *Bookmark*. You will then need to type or paste in the URL (address) for the website you want to save and then can also add a name and description if desired.

Create New Bookmark   ✕

URL

www.onlinecomputertips.com

Name (optional)

Online Computer Tips

Description (optional)

Tech help website

Cancel   **Create**

Figure 2.14

Figure 2.15 shows my saved bookmark with the rest of my files and folders. If I hover my mouse over the information (i) icon, I will be shown the description that I typed in when I created the bookmark.

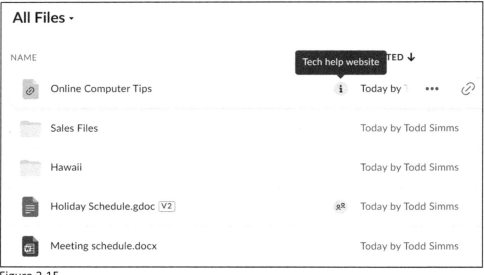

Figure 2.15

Every time I click on the bookmark, my browser will open up that webpage in a new tab. If I need to edit any of the information for that bookmark, I can click on the ellipses (...) to the right of it and choose *More Options* and then *Edit*.

Copying and Moving Files

Once you upload or create a file or folder doesn't mean that is where it must reside. Many times you will find that you need to either copy a file to a different folder or maybe move one altogether. There are a couple of ways you can go about moving or copying files and folders in Box.

To get to the copy and move menus for a file, you can either hover over the file name and then click on the ellipses to view the menu as shown in figure 2.17 or check the box next to a file and then click on ellipses that appears at the upper right of your screen to see the options as shown in figure 2.18.

Figure 2.16

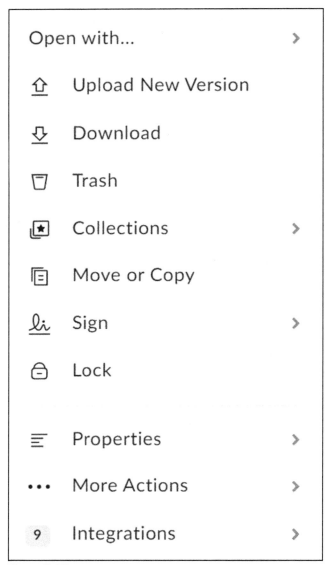

Figure 2.17

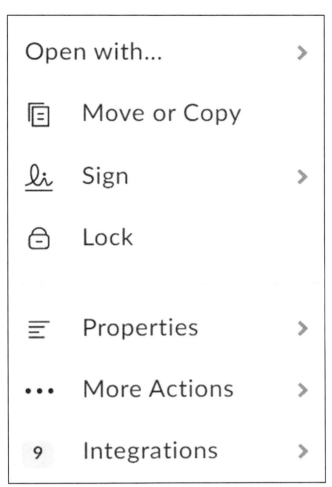

Figure 2.18

Regardless of the method you use, once you click on *Move or Copy*, you will then need to select a destination folder and then either click on the *Move* or *Copy* button depending on what you wish to do with the file.

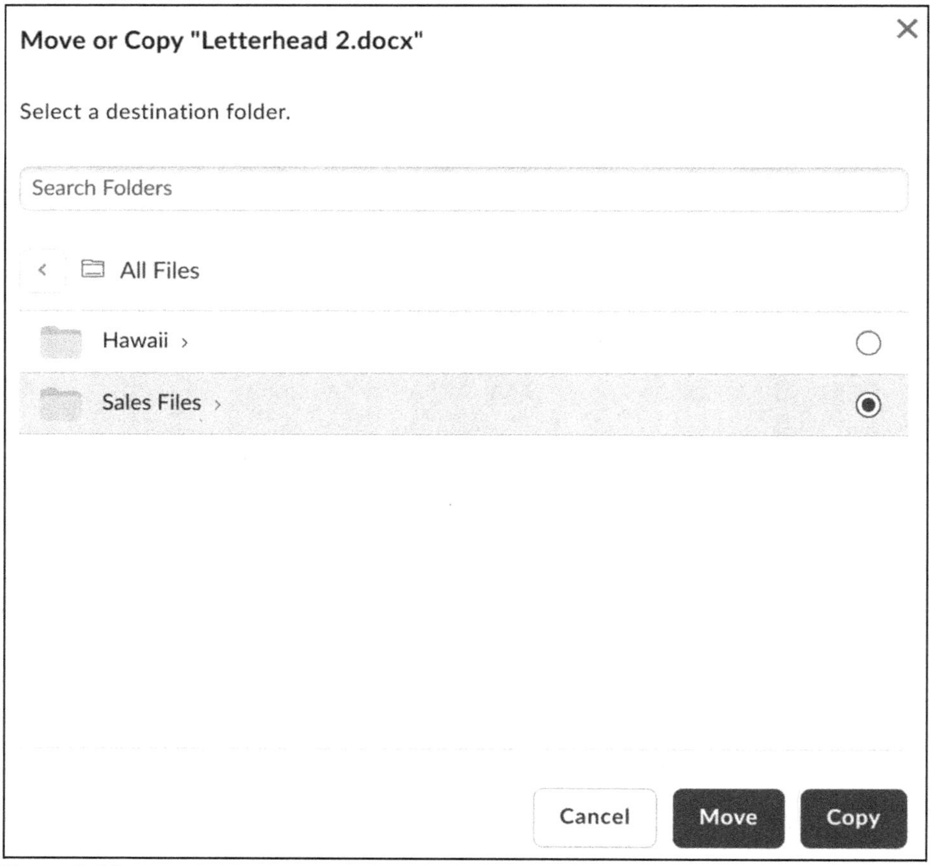

Move or Copy "Letterhead 2.docx"   ✕

Select a destination folder.

> Search Folders

<   🗀 All Files

🗀   Hawaii ›   ○

🗀   Sales Files ›   ◉

Cancel   **Move**   **Copy**

Figure 2.19

After you make your selection, you will then be shown a brief popup where you can undo the move or copy as well as be taken to the new location of the file you moved or copied.

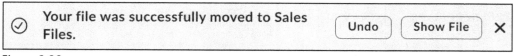

⊘ **Your file was successfully moved to Sales Files.**   Undo   Show File   ✕

Figure 2.20

If you prefer the drag and drop method, you can also drag a file into a new folder just like you did when you dragged files from your desktop into your Box account. Just keep in mind that dragging and dropping files will move them and not copy them and you can do this with more than one file at a time.

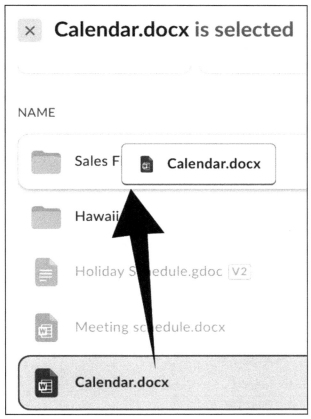

Figure 2.21

These file move and copy procedures will work the same for folders as they do for files. You can also move or copy more than one file at a time by selecting the checkbox next to each one.

Folder Paths

While we are on the subject of moving and copying files, I wanted to take a moment to go over folder paths because they will really help you when it comes to keeping your files organized. Knowing how to manage your files and folders on your computer is one of the most important skills to learn if you want to be proficient when it comes to your day-to-day computer usage.

When you look at the folder structure on your computer, you will notice that it's kind of assembled like a tree that branches off with subfolders as seen in figure 2.22. No matter if you are running Windows, macOS or Linux, you will have a similar folder structure within your operating system.

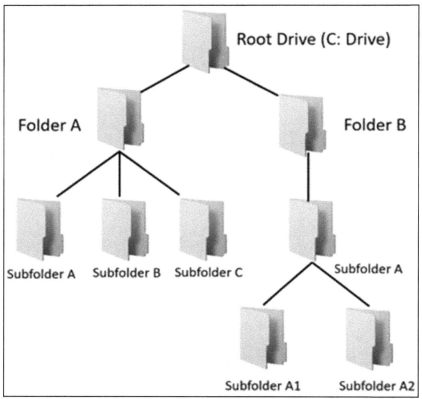

Figure 2.22

If I were to open the Documents folder on my Windows PC and click in the address bar at the top, I would be shown the path to the Documents folder.

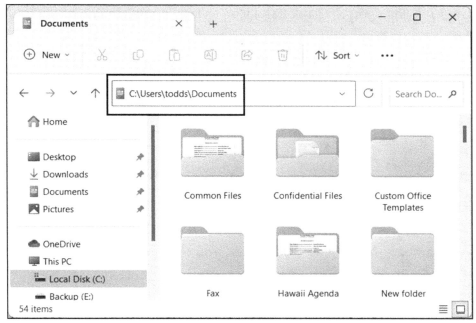

Figure 2.23

Box shows you a similar view as shown in figure 2.24 where I am in my *Confidential Files* folder which is located within my *Sales Files* folder which is then located under *All Files*.

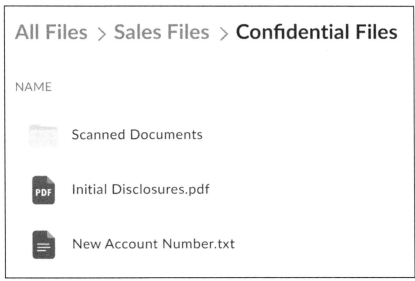

Figure 2.24

If I were to then open the *Scanned Documents* folder within the Confidential Files folder, you can see how the path changes as shown in figure 2.25. When the path gets too long, you will need to click on the icon at the very beginning of the path to see the rest.

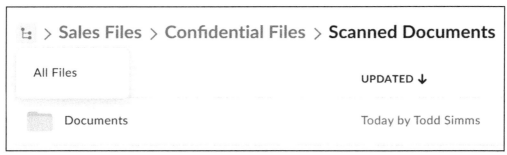

Figure 2.25

If you want to go back to a higher level folder, you can simply click the name of that folder within the path to be taken there.

Renaming Files and Folders

Once you create or upload a file or folder, you are not stuck with its original name and can easily change it whenever necessary.

Once again, there is more than one way to go about the process of renaming a file or folder. The easiest way is to click the pencil icon by the file or folder name and then choose *Rename*. You can also click the ellipses and then go to More Actions and then Rename but why take the extra step?

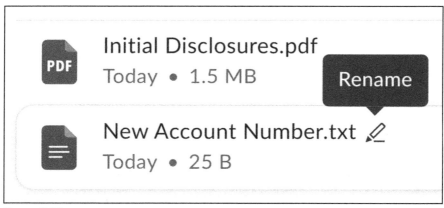

Figure 2.26

Once you click on Rename, all you need to do is type in the new name and click on the *Save* button.

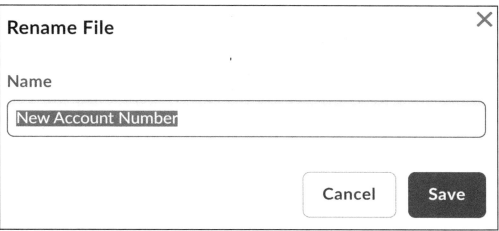

Figure 2.27

Chapter 3 – Working with Your Files and Folders

Cloud storage services such as Box are a great place to store your files for easy access and also as a way to back them up. But if you had to download them every time you wanted to work on them and then re-upload your changes, that would get old rather quickly. Fortunately, Box enables you to edit many different types of files online within your Box account without having to download a copy first.

Working with Files Online

To open a file from your Box account so you can then start working on it, simply click on the file name itself and Box will open the file assuming it's a supported file type. As you can see in figure 3.1, the various files have icons next to their name indicating what online app is associated with the file. When you see these icons, that means Box can most likely open that particular file.

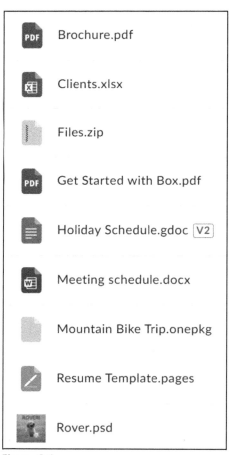

Figure 3.1

If you look at the file named *Mountain Bike Trip.onepkg* in figure 3.1, you will notice that it is a plain grey logo and this usually means Box doesn't have an online app that it can use to open this particular file (more on this later).

If I were to click on the Brochure.pdf file, Box will then open it within my web browser for me to preview. Since it's a PDF file, I will not be able to edit the document but only be able to view it. If I have some type of PDF editing software on my computer, I could then download the file, make my changes, and then re-upload it again.

Figure 3.2

I can also click the *Open* button to get some additional options such as installing Adobe Acrobat for Box.

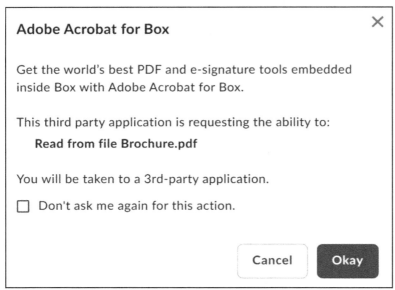

Figure 3.3

When you install an application for Box, you will need to grant that app permission to access your Box account.

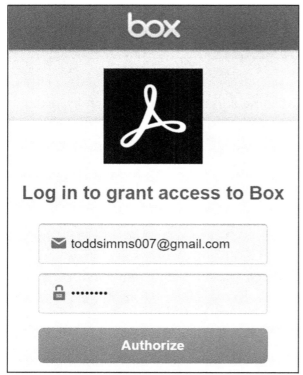

Figure 3.4

In this case, even though I installed Adobe Acrobat for Box, I will still not be able to edit the PDF unless I happen to have a subscription to the professional version of Acrobat.

Now if I were to open a Microsoft Word document by clicking on it, I would still not be able to edit it since it's only a preview of the file but do have the options as shown in figure 3.5.

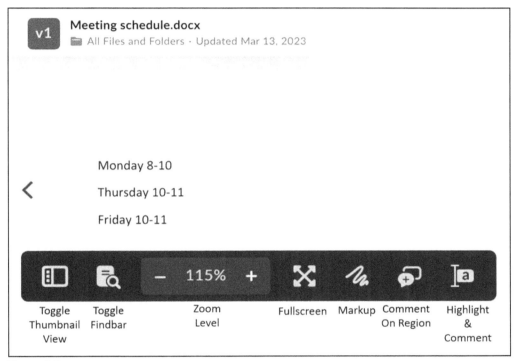

Figure 3.5

Here is what each of these options will do.

- **Toggle thumbnail view** – If there is more than one page to the document, they will be shown as individual thumbnails at the left side of the screen. Then you can click on any page to have it shown in the main viewing area.

- **Toggle Findbar** – This opens a search box where you can type in your search terms.

- **Zoom level** – Here you can zoom in and out of the document to make it larger or smaller.

- **Fullscreen** – This will open the document in a full screen view without any toolbars on the top or sides of the screen.

- **Markup** – If you want to draw some freehand markups, you can use this tool. Then you can add a comment to your markup as needed.

Figure 3.6

Comment on region – This is similar to the Markup option but this time you can draw a box around the section you want to comment on and then type in your comment for others to see.

Figure 3.7

Highlight and comment – This is similar to the Comment on region tool but allows you to highlight a section of the page with a virtual highlighter pen rather than draw a box around an object.

If I want to edit this Word document, I will need to click the *Open* button and choose an app to open the file with. The choices you get will vary depending on the file type and what apps you have installed. Figure 3.8 shows that I can open my document with Microsoft Word Online, Google Docs, or on my desktop using Box Tools (discussed next).

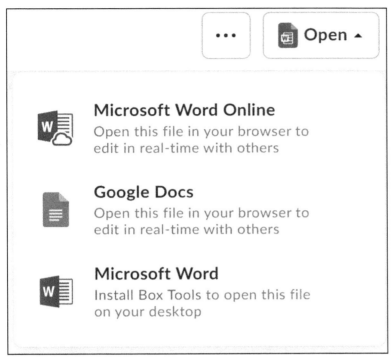

Figure 3.8

If I choose the Microsoft Word Online option, my file will be opened using the online Word app as seen in figure 3.9. I can then edit it as needed and it will be saved in real time. If you look at the upper left corner of the document, you will see that it says *Saved to Box*.

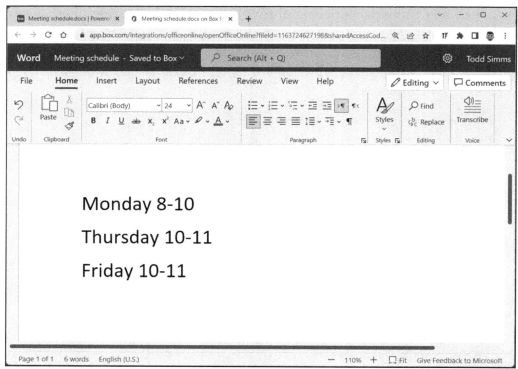

Figure 3.9

If I try to open a file that Box doesn't have an app for such as the *Mountain Bike Trip.onepkg* file I mentioned earlier, I will get a message similar to the one seen in figure 3.10. I will then have to download the file to my computer in order to open it assuming I have the appropriate software installed on my computer to actually open it.

We're sorry, we can't preview this file type in your web browser. To view this content please download and open it on your device.

Download

Figure 3.10

You might also run into a situation where you receive a message similar to that shown in figure 3.11. This usually happens because the type of Box account you have does not allow that type of preview to be shown. For example, you cannot preview movie\video files with the free Box account.

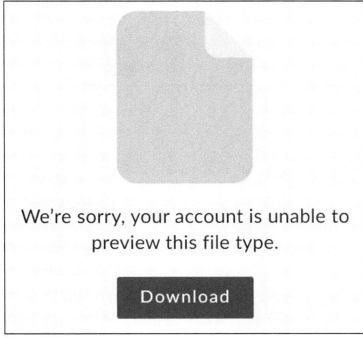

We're sorry, your account is unable to preview this file type.

Download

Figure 3.11

Now if I try to open an Apple Pages document from my Box account, I get a message informing me that I need to enable iWork Previews as seen in figure 3.12. Once I click on *Accept*, my Pages document will open in preview mode and then I will be able to preview other Pages files as needed.

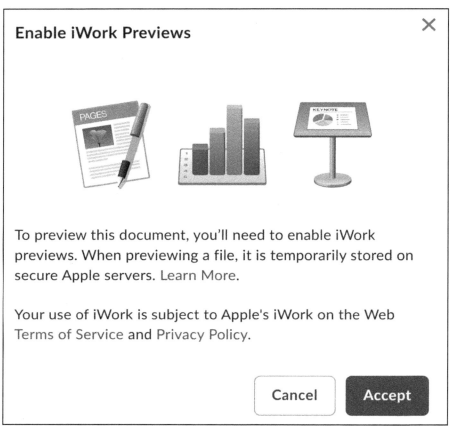

Enable iWork Previews   ✕

To preview this document, you'll need to enable iWork previews. When previewing a file, it is temporarily stored on secure Apple servers. Learn More.

Your use of iWork is subject to Apple's iWork on the Web Terms of Service and Privacy Policy.

Cancel   **Accept**

Figure 3.12

Box Tools

If you would rather open your online documents using your desktop programs such as Microsoft Word or Adobe Acrobat, you can install the Box Tools app to do so. Box Tools is used to open an online file using a program installed on your computer without having to download the file first. Then when you make changes to that document on your computer, the changes will be saved to the file stored in your Box account.

You might have noticed when you click the Open button when accessing a file in your account that you have the option to install box tools as seen at the bottom of figure 3.13.

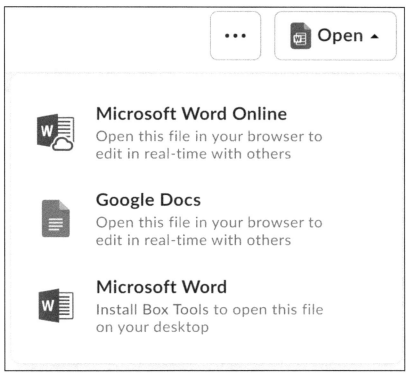

Figure 3.13

If you choose to install Box Tools, you will need to click on the *Download* button and then open the file that will then be downloaded to your computer. You can find the file in the same place where other files you download from the internet are placed. For Windows users, the default is your Downloads folder.

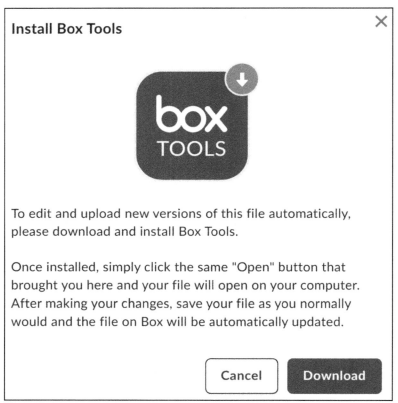

Install Box Tools   ✕

To edit and upload new versions of this file automatically, please download and install Box Tools.

Once installed, simply click the same "Open" button that brought you here and your file will open on your computer. After making your changes, save your file as you normally would and the file on Box will be automatically updated.

Cancel   Download

Figure 3.14

When you open the downloaded file, it will start the installation and it works the same as any other software installation you might have performed in the past. You should be fine with just clicking the *Next* button to go through all the prompts.

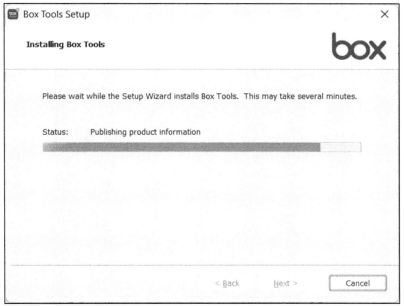

Figure 3.15

After Box Tools is installed and you choose to open the file using your desktop app, you will be shown a message that your file is being opened with that app and that changes will be saved back to Box. You can then click the link that says *Lock file to prevent others from editing it* so that way nobody else changes your file while you are working on the version in your desktop app.

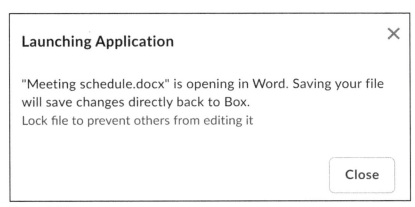

Figure 3.16

Figure 3.17 shows what happens if I were to click on Save as while working on a Word document located in my Box account that was opened using the Word desktop program. As you can see, the path to the document location points to my Box account.

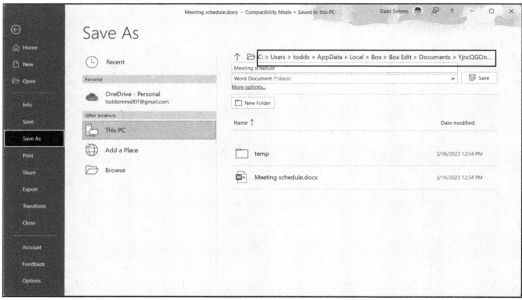

Figure 3.17

One other thing you might notice after working on a document is that you get a popup message telling you that there is a new version of the file available. It then asks you if you want to refresh the page so you will be shown the latest information.

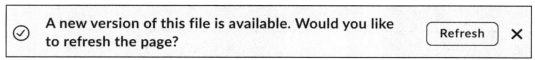

Figure 3.18

File Versions

One common feature you will find with many of the online cloud storage services is the ability to view and revert back to older versions of your files. So let's say you have made some changes to a document over a period of a few weeks and realized that you need to go back to how the document was a week ago. If you had this file stored on your computer, you would be out of luck unless you had made regular backups and used a method that would keep previously changed versions of the file.

If you have one of the Box subscription plans, you can go back to older versions of your files and view and restore them as needed. When you look at the files in your account, you will most likely see some that have V2 or another number after them as seen in figure 3.19.

Figure 3.19

If you were to check the box next to that file and then look at the details section to the right, you would see how many saved versions of the file you have within your account. Figure 3.19 shows that I have two saved versions but if I were to click on the link, I would be shown that I really don't have any saved versions because I am using the free account type for this example (figure 3.20).

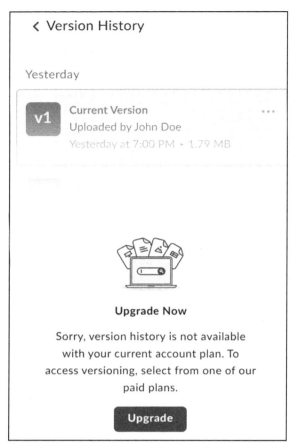

Figure 3.20

Figure 3.21 shows an example of how saved versions look when you have a paid subscription to Box. As you can see, you have the option to preview, download or delete these saved versions of your files. The *Make Current* option is used to have an older version of a file become the latest or most current version of that file. When you use this option, be aware that it will replace the latest version with that older version.

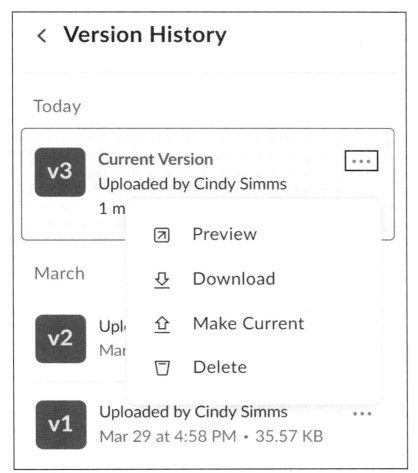

Figure 3.21

Uploading New Versions

If you need to replace a file in your Box account with a new version from your computer, there are several ways to do so. Each of these methods will give you the same results so it's up to you to decide which one works the best for you.

One way to upload a new version of a specific file is to click on the ellipses next to the file name and choose the *Upload New Version* option from the pop-up menu. Then you will need to browse your computer to locate the new version of the file to have it uploaded. Then this newly uploaded file will become the current version.

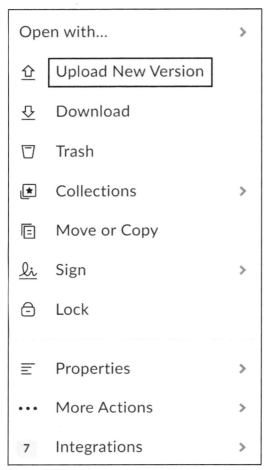

Figure 3.22

Another method you can use is to click on the *New* button and then choose *File Upload* like you would to upload a new file to your account. As long as the file name is exactly the same and you choose to upload it to the same folder in Box, the file will then be replaced with the new version.

Finally, you can use the drag and drop method from your computer into the Box web page. Once again, as long as the file name is exactly the same and you choose to upload it to the same folder in Box, the file will then be replaced with the new version. And if you have a subscription plan that allows for file versions, you will still be able to view or restore the older version of the file if necessary.

Deleting and Undeleting Files and Folders

Just because you have files and folders in your Box account doesn't mean you have to or will want to keep them there forever. Just like with your personal computer, you will always be adding new files and removing files that you no longer need.

The process for deleting files and folders in Box works just like it does on your computer. And if you change your mind and want a file back or deleted it by accident, you can still recover it, as long as you do so in a reasonable amount of time.

To delete a file or folder, simply select it by checking the box next to its name. You can also select multiple items if you want to delete more than one at a time. Once you have the item selected, simply click on the trash can icon that appears at the top of the page.

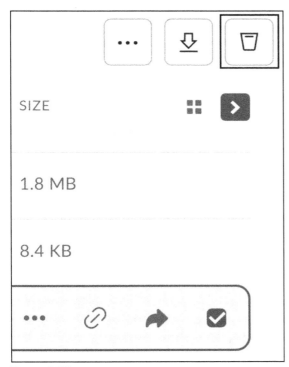

Figure 3.23

You will then be prompted to confirm that you want to delete the item, or you can cancel the deletion process.

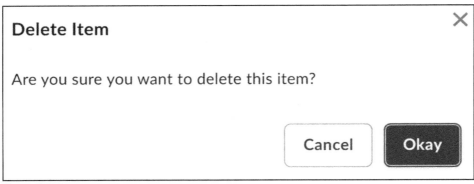

Figure 3.24

Then after you delete the item, you can immediately undo the deletion by clicking the *Undo* button which appears for around five seconds after you click the *Okay* button.

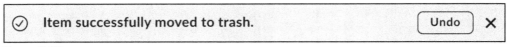

Figure 3.25

Now if you were to go to your Trash section, you would see all of the files and folders that you have recently deleted. Anything in the trash will be permanently deleted after 30 days if you don't restore it. You can see the deleted date and the date that the file or folder will be permanently deleted from this area as well.

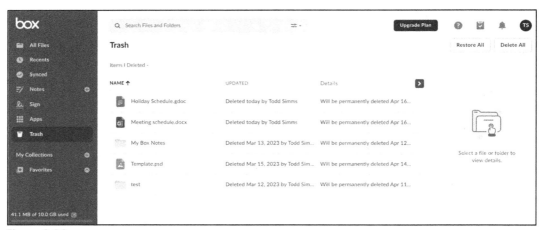

Figure 3.26

At the upper right of the screen, you can also click the button to restore all of the files from the trash to their original location or delete all of the items permanently.

To restore a file, simply click on the ellipses next to its name and then click on *Restore*. The file or folder will be removed from the trash and restored to its original location.

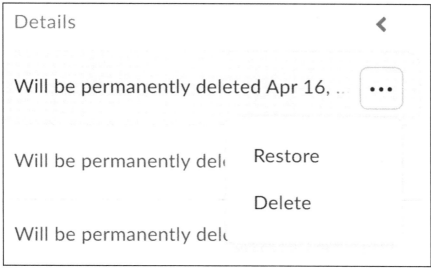

Figure 3.27

Recent Files

You most likely have noticed the *Recent Files* section at the top of your file list when you are in the *All Files* section of Box. This is used to give you quick access to recently used files assuming you will want to open them again. Many people (including myself), think this is mostly a waste of space and fortunately you can close the Recent Files section by clicking the up arrow to the left of the words Recent Files. This will simply minimize this section and you can open it back up again using the same method.

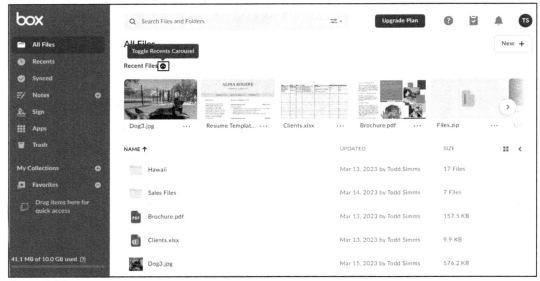

Figure 3.28

When you are not in the All Files section you will not see the Recent Files area at the top of your file list. But if you still want to see or open your recently accessed files, you can do so by clicking on *Recents* over at the left side of the page. This will then open the same recent files, but this time will show you the date you last viewed them.

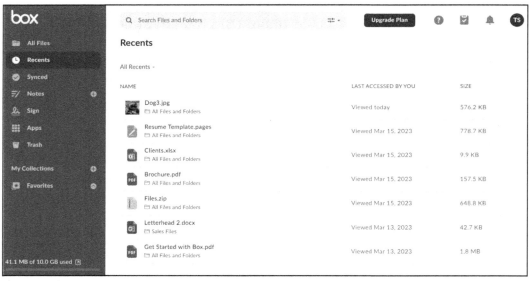

Figure 3.29

Searching For Files and Folders

Once you start using Box for a while and start creating and uploading files and folders, you might find it harder to locate the files that you need to access. Fortunately, Box has a fairly powerful search feature that allows you to find what you are looking for fairly quickly.

At the top of the page you will see a search box where you can type in a word or phrase to look for. As you type your search term, Box will start to show you results based on the letters you are typing. If you find what you are looking for in this list, you can simply click on the result you need to open that file or folder. At the top of this list, you will also see the option to search for only folders with that name or only files with that name.

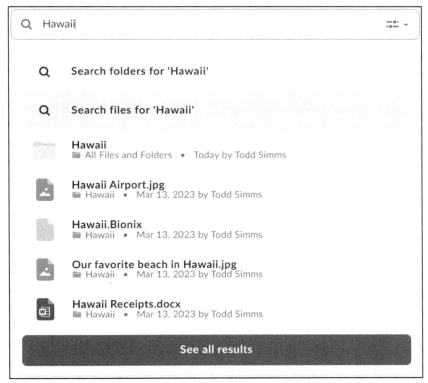

Figure 3.30

If you click on the icon at the right side of the search box, you can filter your search by file type (document, spreadsheet, image, video etc.), date updated and owners of the file. If you haven't done any collaboration with others yet, you will be the only owner of your files and folders.

You may or may not have a use for the Metadata option because that relies on data stored within your files such as the date taken for a photo or the author of a document. To use Metadata with your files, you need to have one of the business accounts and then have a Box administrator set these up.

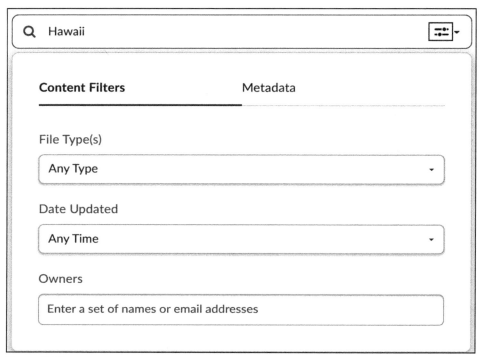

Figure 3.31

If you click on the button at the bottom of the search dropdown list that says *See all results*, you will then be presented with a list of all the files and folders that contain that search term. As you can see in figure 3.32, Box found files and folders that contain the word Hawaii, even if they are just part of a file name or even part of a word such as **Hawaii**an.

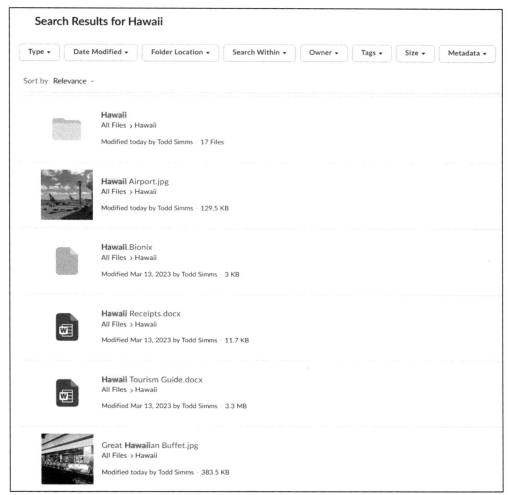

Figure 3.32

At the top of the search results, you will see various filters that you can use to narrow down the search results. So, if you only want to have documents shown, or see files less than 2 MB from the past month that are in a specific folder, you can easily do so using these filters.

I will filter my results to images that are 1MB or less and figure 3.33 shows the results.

Figure 3.33

Locking Files

Once you start sharing your files with others (covered in chapter 4), you might run into an issue where you need to work on a file and need to make sure that no one else can make any changes while you are doing so. This is where locking your files comes into play. When you lock a file, nobody can make changes to that file until you unlock it.

To lock a file, click on the ellipses next to the file name and choose *Lock*. Now you will be able to lock the file until you manually unlock it (unlimited setting), or you can choose a lock duration time as seen in figure 3.35. There is also a checkbox to disable downloading of the file that you can use to ensure nobody can access the file that way as well.

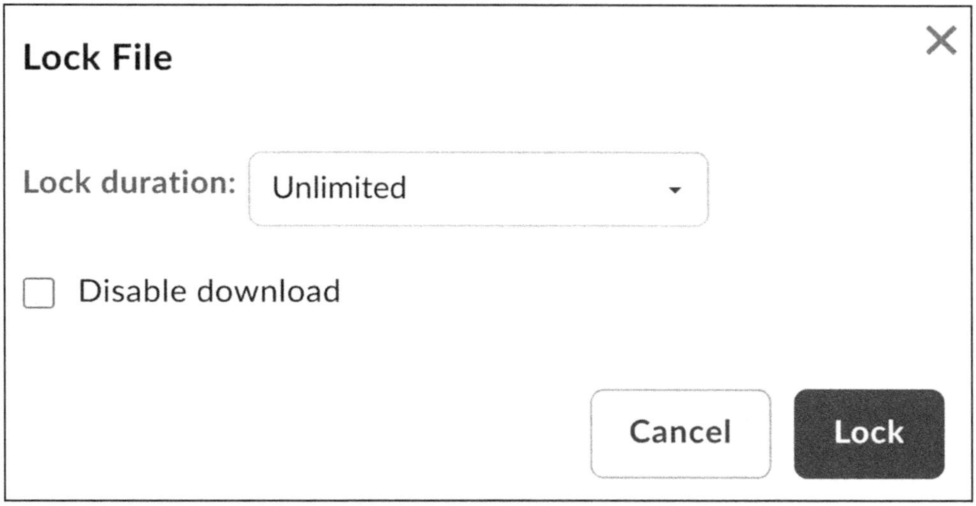

Lock File   ✕

Lock duration: Unlimited   ▼

☐   Disable download

                                          Cancel   **Lock**

Figure 3.34

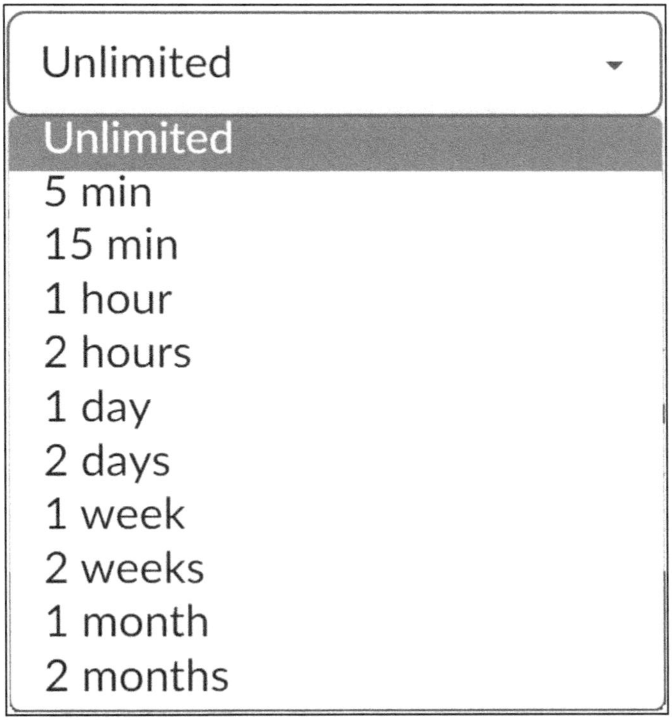

Unlimited   ▼

Unlimited
5 min
15 min
1 hour
2 hours
1 day
2 days
1 week
2 weeks
1 month
2 months

Figure 3.35

After you lock a file, you will have a lock icon next to its name and if you hover your mouse over this icon, it will show you how long the lock duration is set for.

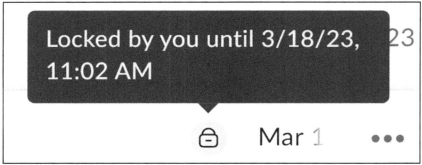

Figure 3.36

When another user tries to access the file, they will see that the *Open* button is greyed out as shown in figure 3.37. The Download button will also be missing if you chose the option to disable downloads.

Figure 3.37

If the person you are sharing the file with has *Editor* level access, they will be able to unlock the file themselves.

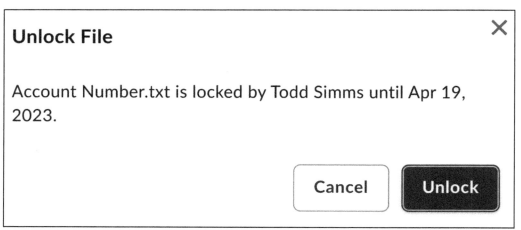

Figure 3.38

If they only have *Viewer* level access, they can request that you unlock the file for them by selecting the *Request Unlock* choice from the file's menu options.

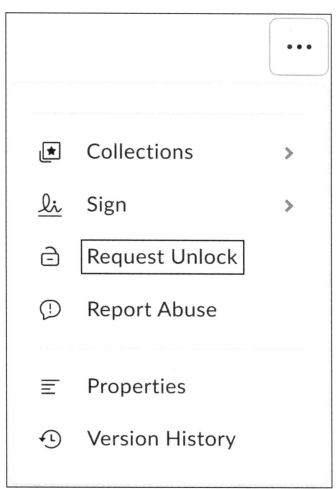

Figure 3.39

When you request to have a file unlocked, you can fill in your reason for the request in the message box and also check the box to have a notification sent to your email once the file has been unlocked.

Request to Unlock   ✕

Account Number.txt is locked by Todd Simms until Mar 18, 2023.

Personal Message (optional)

I need to edit this file today!

☐ Email me when this file is unlocked.

Cancel   **Request Unlock**

Figure 3.40

The owner of the file will then get an email with an option to unlock the file as seen in figure 3.41.

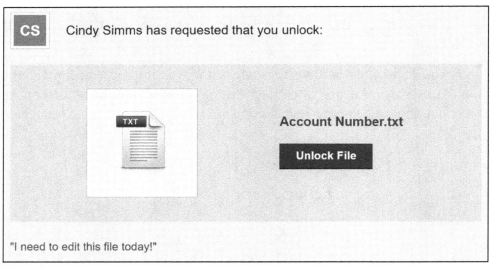

Figure 3.41

Favorites

If you use a web browser (and who doesn't?), then you should be familiar with the concept of favorites or bookmarks as they are also commonly known as. Box has its own favorites section that you can use to give you quick access to your most used files and folder.

To add a file or folder to your Favorites, simply drag it over to the Favorites section on the left side of the screen.

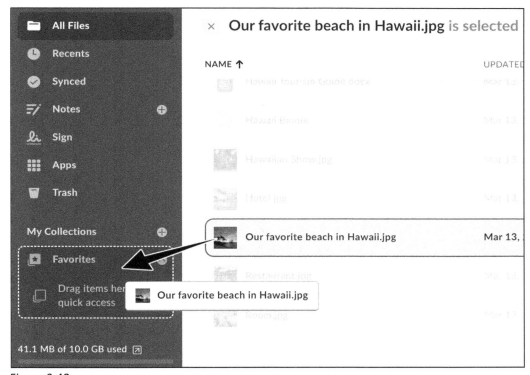

Figure 3.42

Once you have some files and folders in your Favorites, you can click on the Favorites section to view them all in one place. One thing to keep in mind is that the items in your Favorites are still located in their original location so you can think of these files and folders as shortcuts to the originals.

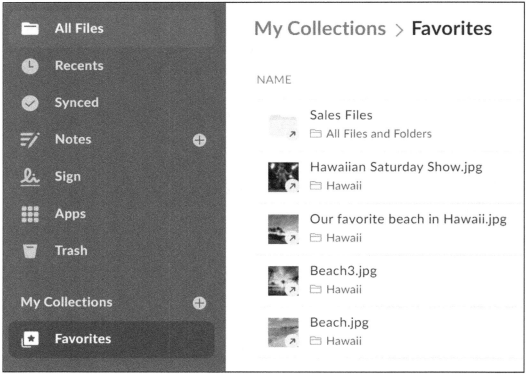

Figure 3.43

If you rename a file, its new name will be updated in your Favorites section. Even if you move a file to a different folder, it will not affect your ability to get to it from your Favorites.

One thing you might notice is that you do not have all the same options for a file or folder such as being able to rename the file or upload a new version. You will need to perform these types of tasks from the file or folder's original location.

To remove a file or folder from your Favorites, simply find it under the Favorites icon on the left side of the screen and click on the X to have it removed. This will not delete the file or folder but simply remove it from the Favorites section.

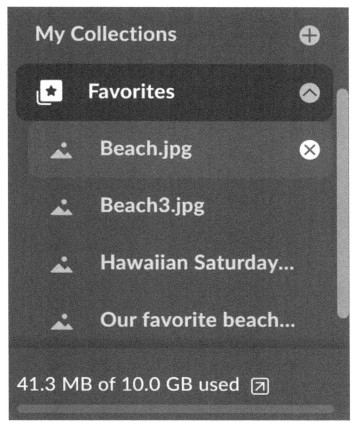

Figure 3.44

The Details Pane

Box offers an easy way to get basic details about your files and folders. This is similar to when you right click a file on your computer and choose the properties option to see information such as its size and date created.

When you select a file or folder, you will be able to view the details of that file or folder on the right side of the screen. If you don't see the details pane when you select a file, then you will need to click on the left pointing arrow to expand it and make it visible.

Figure 3.45

Once you have the details pane open, you will be able to see information such as the file owner, who uploaded it, its created and modified date, and its size (figure 3.46). The description field can be filled in from here if you do not have a description for the file. You will also be able to see a preview of the file if it's a supported file type.

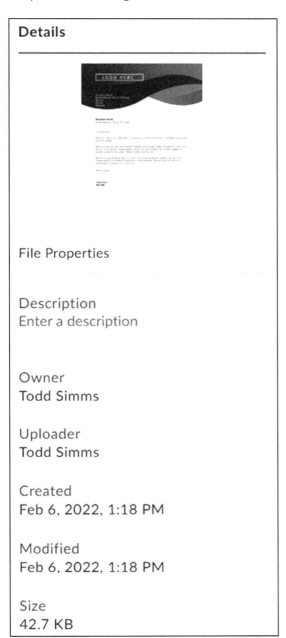

Details

File Properties

Description
Enter a description

Owner
Todd Simms

Uploader
Todd Simms

Created
Feb 6, 2022, 1:18 PM

Modified
Feb 6, 2022, 1:18 PM

Size
42.7 KB

Figure 3.46

If there is more than one version of a file, you will not be shown the file preview but rather how many versions of that file you have saved.

Details

File Properties

2 Saved Versions

Description
Enter a description

Figure 3.47

When you look at the details pane for a folder, you will also have the ability to invite people to access your folder or create a shared link to that folder.

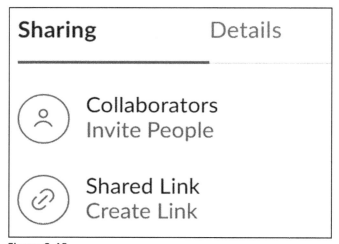

Figure 3.48

You can also view this information for a file when clicking on the ellipses next to the file or folder name and choosing *Properties* and then *File Information*.

Tags
Box allows you to use tags to "tag" files and folders with certain labels to help you do things like mark items with similar properties and filter search results so you only see what you need.

To tag a file or folder, click on the ellipses and choose *More Actions* and then *Add or Edit Tags*.

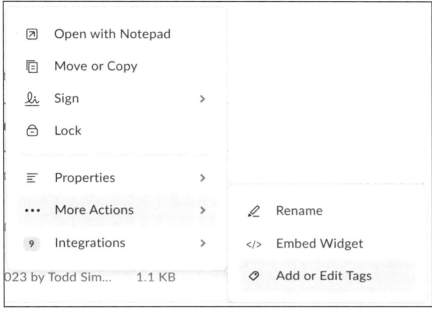

Figure 3.49

Then you can type in as many identifying terms as you need for that item and click the *Save* button.

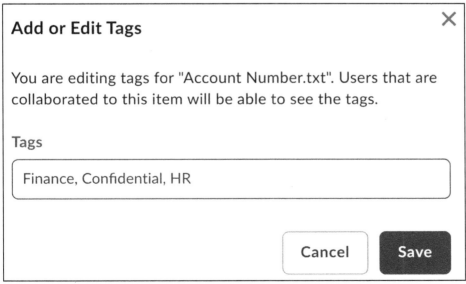

Figure 3.50

After you add tags to your files and folders, the tags will be displayed underneath them, making it easy to see which items have tags associated with them.

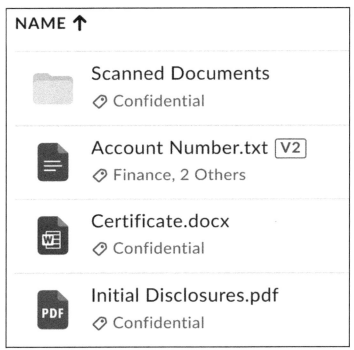

Figure 3.51

As an example, I have added the tag Saturday to some of my Hawaii photos indicating that they were taken on Saturday. If I were to do a search for Hawaii, I would get the results shown in figure 3.52.

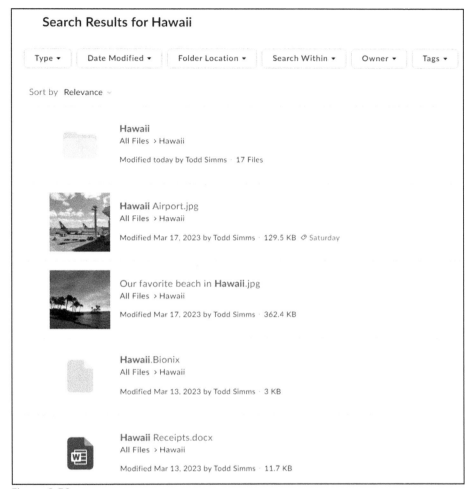

Figure 3.52

To filter my results based on the photos I took on Saturday, I can click the Tags dropdown and type in Saturday to have it only show results based on that tag.

Figure 3.53

I can also click on the Saturday tag next to a file name to accomplish the same thing.

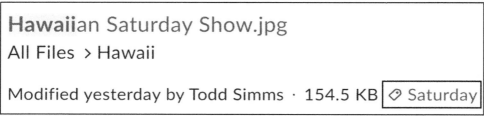

Figure 3.54

Now my results are narrowed down since only the files with the Saturday tag as being displayed.

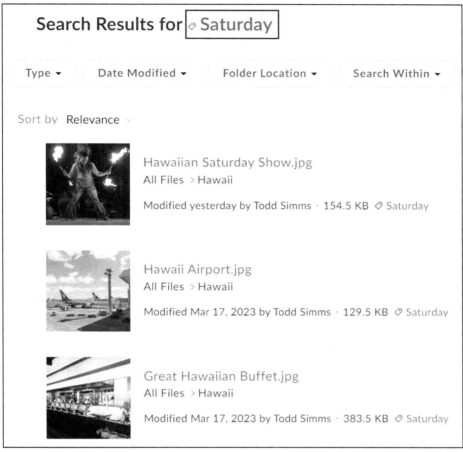

Figure 3.55

Integrations

One nice feature of Box is how it can tie into your other applications to make sending and sharing files easier and faster. If you click on the ellipses next to a file name and then go to the Integrations section, you will see what external applications you can use with your Box account. Figure 3.56 shows the choices for files while figure 3.57 shows the choices for folders. Your choices might differ depending on what apps you have associated with your account. I will be discussing Box apps in chapter 5.

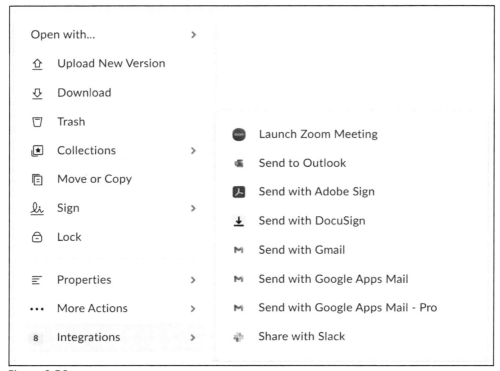

Figure 3.56

Figure 3.57

For my example, I will be using the *Send to Outlook* integration choice to share a PDF file. Once I click on Send to Outlook, I will be shown a message explaining what will happen if I use this method.

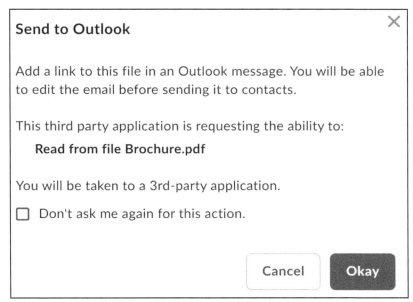

Figure 3.58

Once I click Okay, I will be shown the file that I am sharing and then the permission level if applicable.

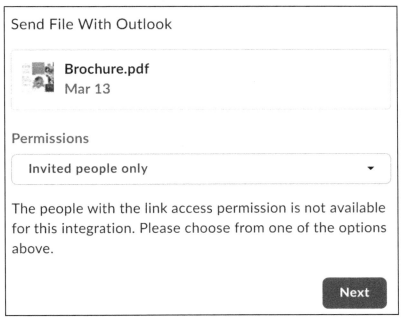

Figure 3.59

Next, I will need to sign into my Microsoft account since that is what will be used to access my Outlook email account.

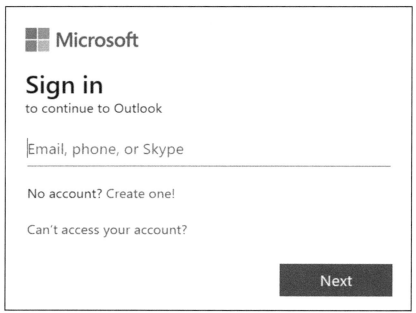

Figure 3.60

Figure 3.61 shows my PDF file attached as a link in the email. Now I just need to add any recipients and type any additional message I wish to send with the file.

Figure 3.61

When the recipient(s) gets the email, they can then click on the link to open the file that I have shared with them.

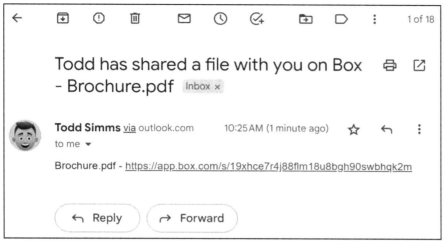

Figure 3.62

If they click the file link and get a message similar to figure 3.63, that is because of how this particular integration handles sharing.

Figure 3.63

If you refer back to figure 3.59, you will see that it says that *the people with the link access permission is not available for this integration* and that the *invited people only* option is the only one that can be used. So if the person I sent this link to was not on the invited people list, they would not be able to view the file.

To get around this, I can go to the share properties of the PDF file and change it from *Invited people only* to *People with the link* (figures 3.64 and 3.65). I will be discussing sharing in more detail in chapter 4.

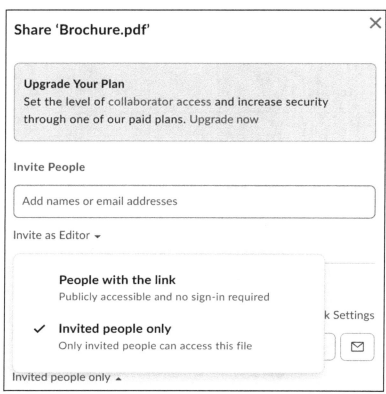

Figure 3.64

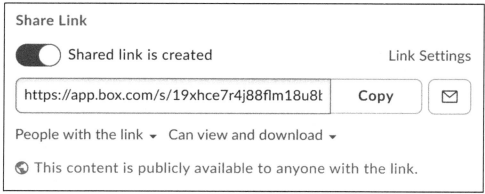

Figure 3.65

Collections

The Collections feature in Box is used as a method where you can store files, folders and links that you would like grouped together. You can think of a collection as a container for items that all fall into the same category such as pictures of your dog or documents for a school project.

When you create a collection, you are not moving these items from their original location into a new location. A collection allows you to store shortcuts to these files etc. in one place similar to how the favorites feature works. But the main difference between a collection and a favorite is that a collection can contain multiple items whereas a favorite is just one document or folder etc.

To create a Collection, simply click the **+** button next to the word Collections in the side navigation panel on the left. I will be making a collection for this year's upcoming trip back to Hawaii so I will call my collection *Upcoming Hawaii Vacation*.

Figure 3.66

One thing you will notice after creating a collection is that it will be listed under the *My Collections* section just like your favorites are under the Favorites section. If you have your Favorites expanded, it might look as though your collection is under this category, but it is actually under the My Collection section.

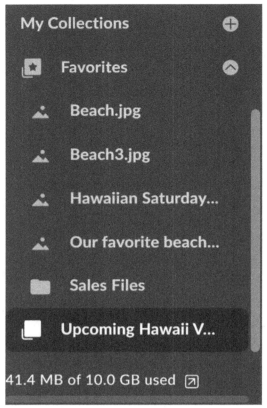

Figure 3.67

To view a collection, you will need to click on *My Collections* itself which will open your collections in a new window. You will also notice that your Favorites are listed here as well. You can click on the ellipses next to your collection to rename it or delete it.

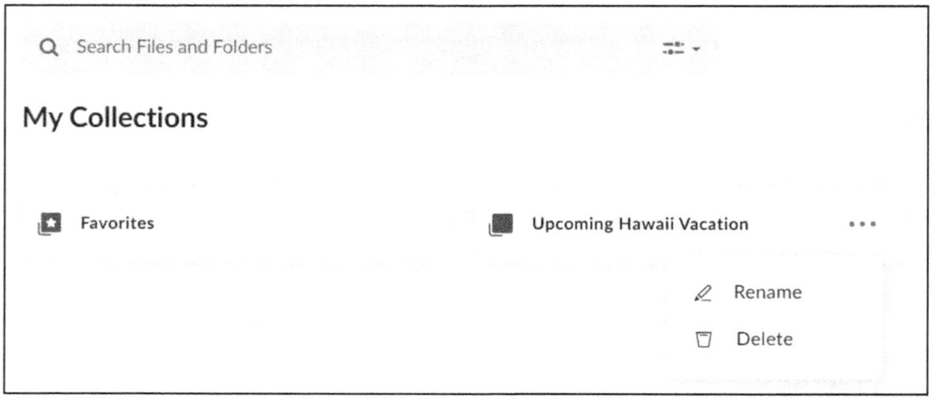

Figure 3.68

Clicking on the collection itself will open it up to show you what items you have added to it. Since I have not added anything yet, I am shown the message from figure 3.69.

Add items to this empty collection

Whenever you have an item selected or are previewing an item in Box and see the icon above, click to Add the item or folder to a Collection.

Also, when you have an item or folder selected in All Files, simply drag & drop the item row to this collection in the lefthand sidebar.

Figure 3.69

There are several ways to add an item to a collection. You can click on the ellipses next to that item and then choose *Collections* and then check the collection you want to add it to.

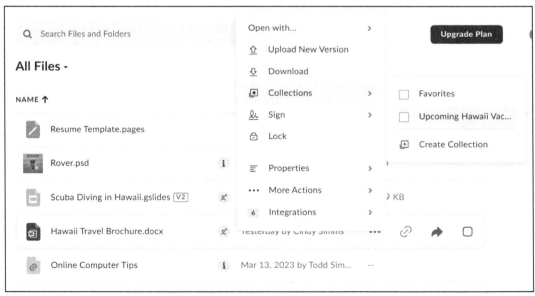

Figure 3.70

You can also drag and drop an item to your collection in the side navigation section. Or when you have a file open, you can also click on the ellipses and choose Collections and then the appropriate collection once again.

Once you have added items to a collection, you will see the collection name underneath that item indicating that it is part of a collection. As you can see in figure 3.71, I have added some files that were shared with me by Cindy Simms to my collection, so these items do not have to be only those that you have created or own.

	Rover.psd	i	Mar 15, 2023 by Todd Sim...	6 MB
	Scuba Diving in Hawaii.gslides [V2] ⬜ Upcoming Hawaii Vacation	℘	Yesterday by Cindy Simms	731.9 KB
	Hawaii Travel Brochure.docx ⬜ Upcoming Hawaii Vacation	℘	Yesterday by Cindy Simms	2.1 MB

Figure 3.71

I have added some additional files as well as a folder and website bookmark to my collection and the results are shown in figure 3.72. Now everything I need for my upcoming trip back to Hawaii is in one place even though I have not moved anything from its original location.

My Collections > **Upcoming Hawaii Vacation**		
NAME	UPDATED ↓	SIZE
Hawaii Videos □ Hawaii	Today by Todd Simms	0 Files
Hawaii Chopper Tours Website □ Hawaii	Yesterday by Todd Simms	--
Scuba Diving in Hawaii.gslides V2 □ All Files and Folders	Yesterday by Cindy Simms	731.9 KB
Hawaii Travel Brochure.docx □ All Files and Folders	Yesterday by Cindy Simms	2.1 MB
Hawaii Receipts.docx □ Hawaii	Mar 13, 2023 by Todd Sim...	11.7 KB
Hawaii Tourism Guide.docx □ Hawaii	Mar 13, 2023 by Todd Sim...	3.3 MB
Room.jpg □ Hawaii	Mar 13, 2023 by Todd Sim...	71.1 KB

Figure 3.72

Box Drive Desktop App

If you have used any of the other cloud storage services such as DropBox or Google Drive, you might have also used their desktop client software to make it easier to copy and sync files between your computer and online storage account.

Box has their own desktop app that you can download for free and then install on your computer. All you need to do to get the software is go to their download page and then download it like you would any other online file. There is a Windows and a Mac version depending on what operating system you are running on your computer.
https://www.box.com/resources/downloads

Once you download the file, simply double-click it to start the installation. The software will install fairly quickly and then you should have a Box icon on your desktop.

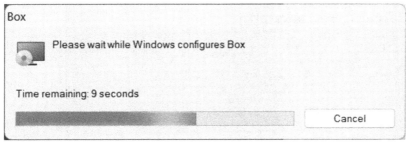

Figure 3.73

The first time you run the software, you will need to log in with your Box credentials just like you do for the website.

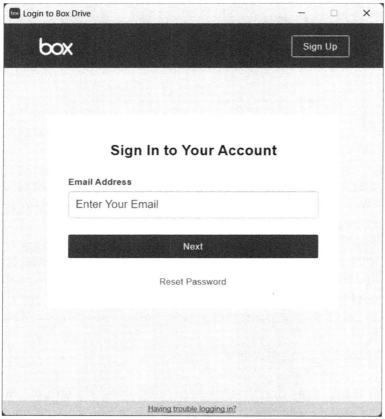

Figure 3.74

Then you should see an overview screen that you can scroll through which will tell you what you can do with the Box client (Box Drive).

Figure 3.75

When you open the Box Drive app, you will see the same files and folders that you have stored online, and they will also have cloud icons next to them indicating that they are online files and folders.

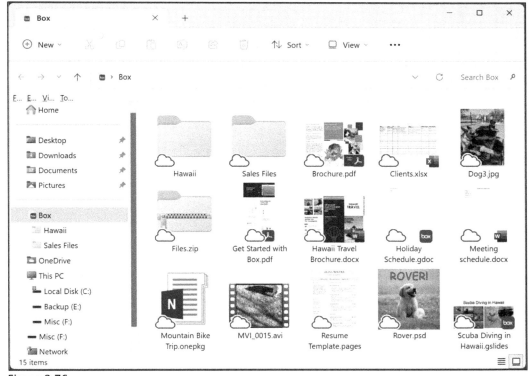

Figure 3.76

Now if I were to drag and drop or copy and paste a file called *Agenda.docx* into my new Box Drive on my desktop, its icon would first have a sync symbol next to it as seen in figure 3.79. Then it would turn into a cloud symbol after it was uploaded to my online account.

Agenda.docx

Figure 3.77

Now if I go back to my Box account online, I will see my newly added file with the other files I currently have in my account. If I were to copy the file to one of my folders in the Box Drive software, it would show up in that same folder online.

All Files ▾

Recent Files ◉

NAME ↑	UPDATED	SIZE
Hawaii	Yesterday by Todd Simms	18 Files
Sales Files □ Favorites	Mar 19, 2023 by Todd Sim...	7 Files
Agenda.docx	Today by Todd Simms	49 KB
Brochure.pdf	Mar 13, 2023 by Todd Sim...	157.5 KB

Figure 3.78

Now if I were to open this file from the Box folder on my computer and make some changes and save it, the new version would be reflected in my Box account online.

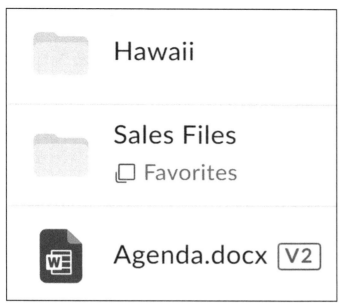

Figure 3.79

Of course you can open a file from your Box Drive and do a save as and save a separate copy somewhere else on your computer. You can also delete files from Box Drive and they will be removed from your online storage as well.

To have a file or folder sync automatically from your Box online account to your desktop, you can check the box next to it and then go to the Details pane and enable the Sync to Desktop feature.

Figure 3.80

This will also automatically sync any subfolders within that folder, but you do have the option to go to the Details pane for a subfolder and turn off the sync setting for that folder.

You can then go to the Synced section online and view all the folders that are set up to sync with your desktop.

Figure 3.81

Chapter 4 – Sharing and Collaborating

One of the biggest reasons for using a cloud storage account is the ability to easily share files with others rather than having to email them to the people who need to view or work on them. Imagine if you had a document that five people were working on and you had to email back and forth between all five people and hope that you had the most current version when it was your turn to make changes.

Online cloud storage services like Box allow you to share these files and work on them online so that you always have access to the most current version. Plus, you don't need to worry about having multiple versions of the same file within multiple emails in your inbox getting everyone confused.

In this chapter, I will be discussing the sharing process and how you can use it to collaborate with other people to ensure everyone on your team has the information they need, and that this information is up to date at all times.

Sharing

One of the main reasons for using an online cloud storage service is the ability to share your files with other people to give them an easy way to your files as well as the ability to see any updates you make to these files.

When sharing files and folders, you will need to decide if you just want others to view them or be able to do things such as edit your files or add (or remove) files to your folders etc.

The easiest way to share a file or folder is to either click the *Share* arrow button by the file name as shown in figure 4.1 or click the Share button while viewing a file as seen in figure 4.2.

Figure 4.1

Figure 4.2

When sharing a file or folder you will have the option to invite people or create a shared link that you can then send via an email or instant message etc.

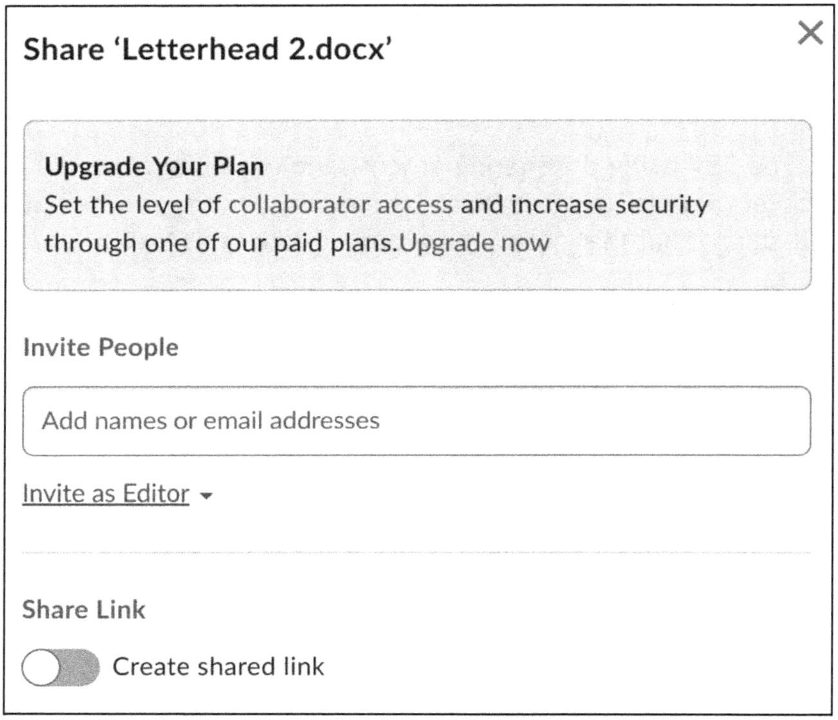

Share 'Letterhead 2.docx'   ✕

Upgrade Your Plan
Set the level of collaborator access and increase security through one of our paid plans.Upgrade now

Invite People

Add names or email addresses

Invite as Editor ▾

Share Link

⚪ Create shared link

Figure 4.3

The *Invite People* section is where you would type in the email addresses of the people you want to share the file with. Then the recipient would receive an email similar to the one shown in figure 4.4. To access the file, they would simply click on the *Go to File* button to be taken directly to it. If they are not logged into their Box account, they would need to do so. If they do not have a Box account, they would need to create one before being able to access the file.

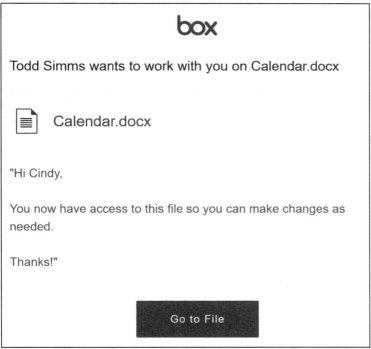

Figure 4.4

As you can see in figure 4.5, the email looks similar when sharing a folder.

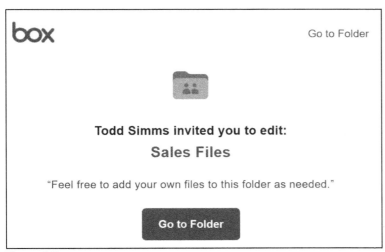

Figure 4.5

If you are unsure if the people you want to share your file with have a Box account or are not concerned about who is able to view or edit your file, you can create a shared link instead of inviting people. Once you enable the shared link you can simply click the *Copy* button and then paste it into an email, or you can click the envelope button to bring up a box where you can add their email addresses and have Box send them an email for you (figure 4.7).

Share Link

Shared link is created   Link Settings

https://app.box.com/s/9ynl3skdeo5ea86kf6q7   **Copy**   ✉

People with the link ▾   Can view and download ▾

🌐 This content is publicly available to anyone with the link.

Figure 4.6

Email Shared Link

Add names or email addresses

Message (optional)

Add a message

Cancel   **Send**

Figure 4.7

If you want to change the access level of your shared link you can do so from two places. You can click the up arrow next to *People with the link* to change it from People with the link to *Invited people only* meaning they will need to receive an email invitation from you sent from Box in order to access the file or folder.

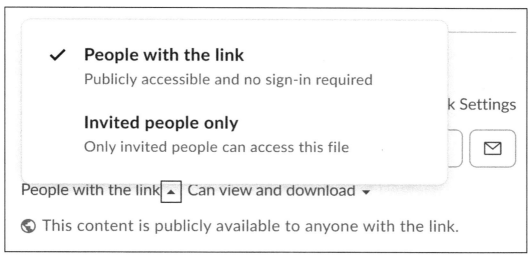

Figure 4.8

You can also click the up arrow next to *Can view and download* to change it to *Can edit* or *Can view only* depending on your needs.

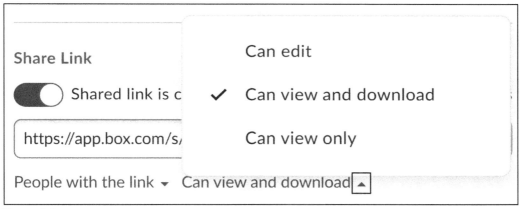

Figure 4.9

Figure 4.10 shows how a shared link appears when configured with the default options of *People with the link* and *Can view and download*. As you can see, there is a message saying you need to log into Box to save it to your own Box account but there is also a *Download* button indicating this file can be saved to their PC.

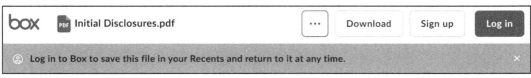

Figure 4.10

Collaborators

Sharing files and folders is one step in the collaboration process but making sure the right people have access to the right files and folders is another step and also so you can see who is working on what file. You also need to make sure they have the correct permissions so they can do what they need to do yet not more than they should be doing! Think of collaborators as people you manually invite to a shared file or folder rather than simply send a shared link to.

Going back to the interface you see when you share a file or folder, you can see that if you have one of the higher-level plans, you will have additional access levels compared to the free plan which only includes Editor and Viewer.

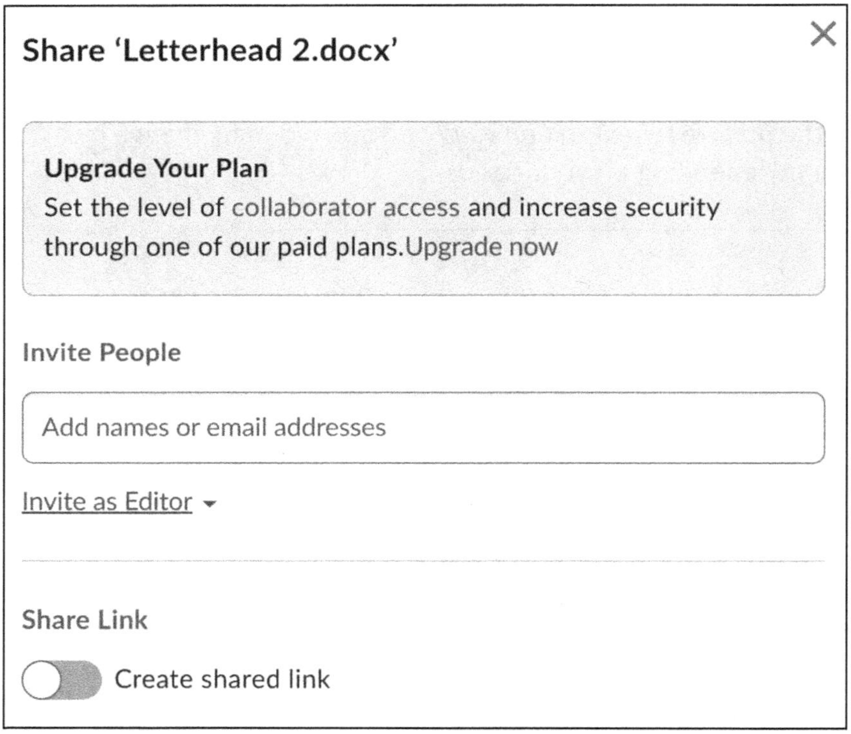

Figure 4.11

Here are the available access levels which will vary depending on the plan you have. You can check the Box website for details about what collaborator level has what permissions.

- Co-owner
- Editor
- Viewer-Uploader

- Previewer-Uploader
- Viewer
- Previewer
- Uploader

As you share your files and folders, you should try and assign the right permission levels to your collaborators, so you don't have to come back and change things later. Of course, it's easy to change permission levels but by the time you realize it, someone might have made a change they shouldn't have or even deleted a file that you didn't want to be deleted.

When a folder has been shared with you, it will appear as a grey color with a globe icon on it, rather than the default yellow color you normally see. And if you hover your mouse over the folder, it will say *External Folder* meaning it's shared with you and is not local to your account.

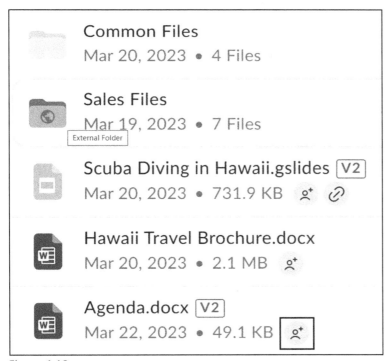

Figure 4.12

For shared files, you will have an icon next to its name with a silhouette figure and a plus sign. You can then click on this icon to see who has permission to view or edit this file and when they were added. If you have the appropriate permission, you can change your permission level and even remove yourself from the shared file. You can also get to this screen by clicking on the ellipses next to a file and then choosing *More Actions > Manage Collaborators*.

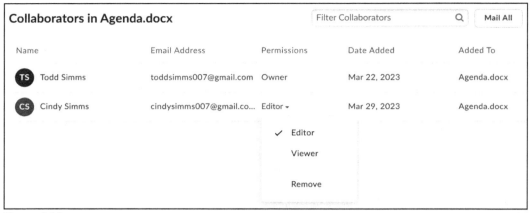

Figure 4.13

Another way to remove yourself from a shared file or folder is to click the ellipses next to that item and then choose *More Actions > End Collaboration*.

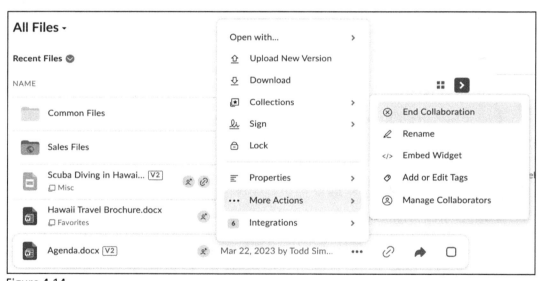

Figure 4.14

Activity

Once you have files and folders shared and have a handle on who you are sharing these items with, you can then monitor how your collaborators are making changes to your shared files to ensure they are doing only what they should be doing with them.

When looking at your files, you might notice an icon next to the file name that looks similar to the one you saw for shared files but this time it will have two silhouette figures on it instead of just one. Then if you hover your mouse over this icon, you will be told that the file is being edited, meaning someone else on your team has the file open and is working on it. Or they might have just left it open and are not doing anything with it at the moment.

Figure 4.15

Just because someone else has a file open, doesn't mean you can't open it yourself to either view or edit that file as well (assuming you have Editor permission). When another person is working on the file or has made a change, you will see it indicated by a marker next to where they were working. This might be noted differently depending on what app you are opening the file with. Figure 4.16 shows how it looks in Word Online and figure 4.17 shows how it looks in Google Docs.

Figure 4.16

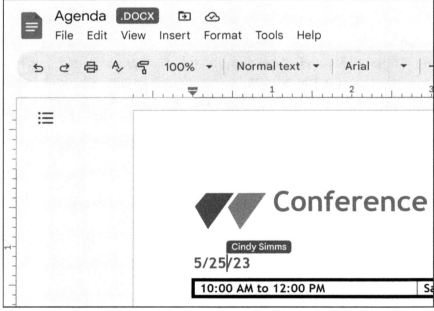

Figure 4.17

One thing you might also notice when you try and open a file using a desktop application such as Microsoft Word is that it won't let you because that requires the file to be downloaded and opened on your computer. When you open a file this way, nobody else can work on it at the same time so if it's already in use by someone else, you will not be able to work on it using your desktop app.

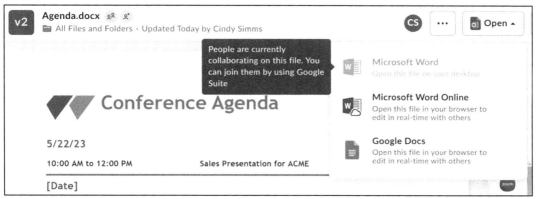
Figure 4.18

If you still want to work on the file on your computer itself, you are still able to download the file so you can use your desktop app that way. Just keep in mind that once you upload your changes, you will be overwriting any changes that were made since you downloaded the file, assuming there was anyone else working on the file.

To check the activity of a file, you can open its preview by clicking on the file name itself and then go to the *Activity* section. Here you will be shown a brief overview of what has been happening with your file. As you can see in figure 4.19, it shows that 2 collaborators uploaded versions 1 through 5.

Figure 4.19

At the top of the preview window, you will see the initials of the last person to work on the file as seen in figure 4.20. If you click on their initials, you will see a more detailed view of the activity taken on that file.

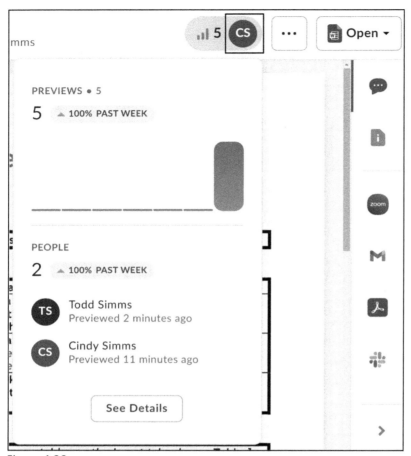

Figure 4.20

Clicking on the *See Details* button will show you additional details about the file activity. You can also see the details broken down in the last week, month, three months or year by choosing the time period at the top of the window.

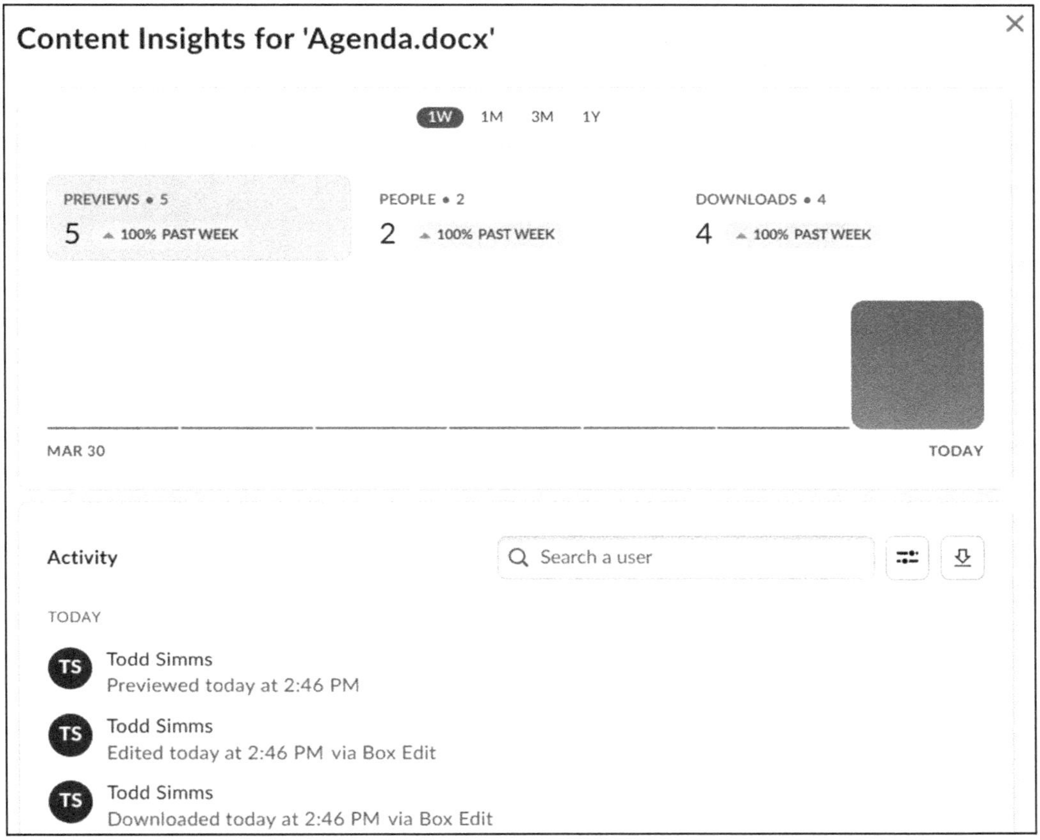

Content Insights for 'Agenda.docx'

1W 1M 3M 1Y

PREVIEWS • 5
5 ▲ 100% PAST WEEK

PEOPLE • 2
2 ▲ 100% PAST WEEK

DOWNLOADS • 4
4 ▲ 100% PAST WEEK

MAR 30   TODAY

Activity   🔍 Search a user

TODAY

TS Todd Simms
Previewed today at 2:46 PM

TS Todd Simms
Edited today at 2:46 PM via Box Edit

TS Todd Simms
Downloaded today at 2:46 PM via Box Edit

Figure 4.21

If you want to export the activity for a file, you can click on the down arrow as seen in figure 4.21 and then choose which events, users and time period you want to save.

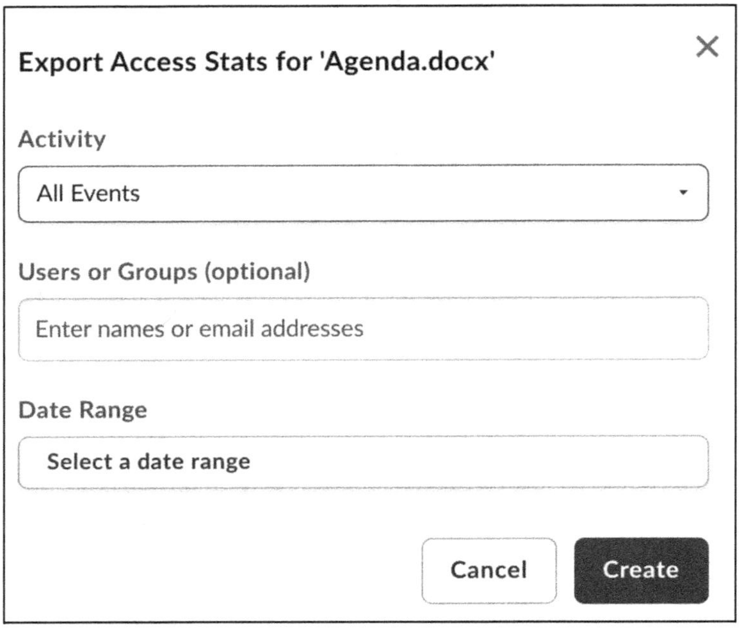

Export Access Stats for 'Agenda.docx'   ✕

Activity

All Events   ▾

Users or Groups (optional)

Enter names or email addresses

Date Range

Select a date range

Cancel   **Create**

Figure 4.22

Once you click the *Create* button, you will see a popup message telling you that your report is being generated and you can click on the *Go to Folder* button to be taken to the location of your report.

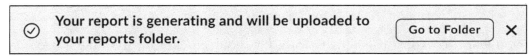

✓ **Your report is generating and will be uploaded to your reports folder.**   Go to Folder   ✕

Figure 4.23

If you are unable to click the Go to Folder button in time, then you can go to your All Files section and click on the *Box Reports* folder. Within this folder you will have other folders named after the report you have run. You will also receive an email with a link to this folder.

All Files > Box Reports

NAME ↑

📁 Access Stats for Agenda.docx run on 2023-04-05 15-08-24

Figure 4.24

When you open the folder, you will see a description of that report type and will also have a CSV (Comma Separated Values) file in that folder for the report.

> ⊛ **Folder Description**
> Status: Completed
> Report Type: Access Stats
> Date Range: 2023-04-05 to 2023-04-05
> Run On: 2023-04-05 15:08:24
> File name: Agenda.docx
>
>
> NAME ↑
>
>
> ▦   access_stats_for_agenda.docx_run_on_2023-04-05-15-08-24_Page_1....

Figure 4.25

If you click on the CSV file, you will see a preview of the file (figure 4.26). If you were to open the file, there is a good chance that your computer would use its built-in text editor app such as Notepad for Windows which will not display the contents of the file in an easy-to-read format.

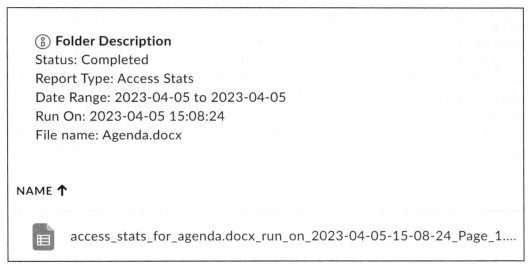

Figure 4.26

What you can do is download the file and then open it with a spreadsheet program such as Microsoft Excel as seen in figure 4.27.

	A	B	C	D	E	F
3	4/5/2023 14:46	Todd Simms	toddsimms007@gmail.com	Edits	Agenda.docx	Service: Box Edit
4	4/5/2023 14:46	Todd Simms	toddsimms007@gmail.com	Downloads	Agenda.docx	Service: Box Edit
5	4/5/2023 14:44	Todd Simms	toddsimms007@gmail.com	Previews	Agenda.docx	Service: Box Elements (used in Box Web App)
6	4/5/2023 14:44	Todd Simms	toddsimms007@gmail.com	Edits	Agenda.docx	Service: Box for Office Online Internal Upload Service
7	4/5/2023 14:44	Todd Simms	toddsimms007@gmail.com	Downloads	Agenda.docx	Service: Box for Office for web
8	4/5/2023 14:44	Todd Simms	toddsimms007@gmail.com	Downloads	Agenda.docx	Service: Box for Office for web
9	4/5/2023 14:44	Todd Simms	toddsimms007@gmail.com	Previews	Agenda.docx	Service: Box Elements (used in Box Web App)
10	4/5/2023 14:38	Todd Simms	toddsimms007@gmail.com	Previews	Agenda.docx	Service: Box Elements (used in Box Web App)
11	4/5/2023 14:38	Cindy Simms	cindysimms007@gmail.com	Edits	Agenda.docx	Service: Box Edit
12	4/5/2023 14:37	Cindy Simms	cindysimms007@gmail.com	Downloads	Agenda.docx	Service: Box Edit
13	4/5/2023 14:37	Cindy Simms	cindysimms007@gmail.com	Previews	Agenda.docx	Service: Box Elements (used in Box Web App)

Figure 4.27

Notifications

If you have a smartphone, then you are familiar with the concept of notifications since you most likely receive them all day long! Box will also send you notifications from time to time and you will see them next to the bell icon at the upper right corner of the page.

Figure 4.28

When you click on the notification bell icon, it will clear the number next to it and also show you all of the notifications that were available to you at that time.

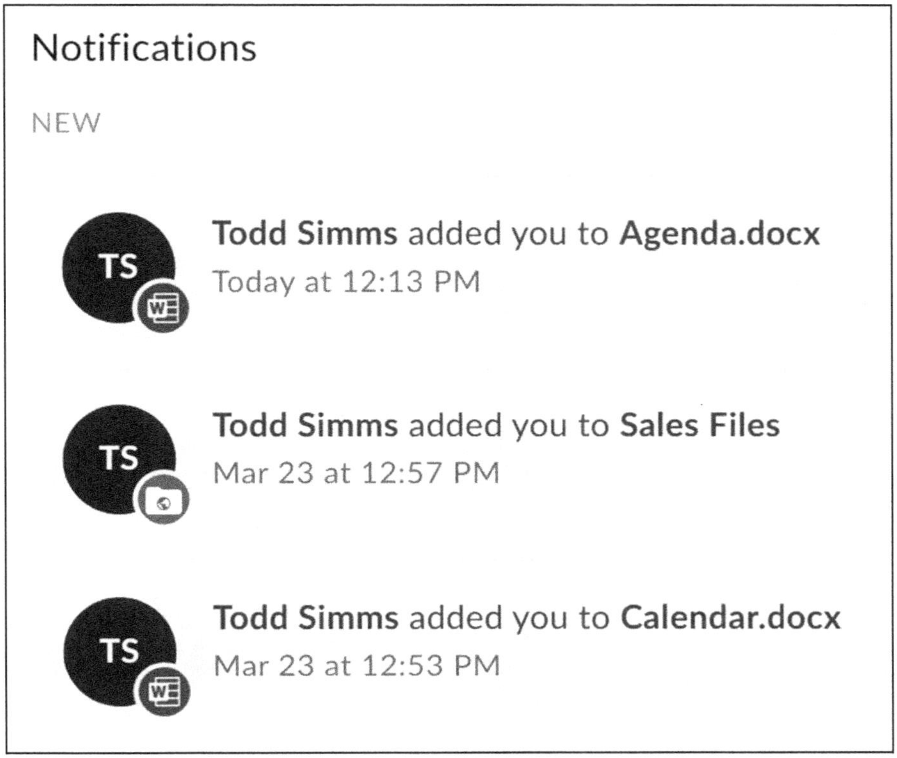

Figure 4.29

You can then click on any one of the notifications to be taken to that file in case you want to check out any changes that were made.

Comments

If you have used any other file sharing platforms such as Google Docs, you might be familiar with the concept of adding comments to documents as you work on them. Box has a similar feature where you can leave comments on files so others can read what you have to say about them. This is a little different than leaving a comment within a document itself because with Box, you can't add a comment to a specific part within a document or other file but rather just on the file itself.

When previewing a file, you can go to the activity section and then you will see the *Write a comment* section at the bottom where you can type in your comment. You will notice that you can mention someone specific in a comment by typing the @ symbol and then their name. Box should suggest the name for you as you are typing it in, so you get the right format.

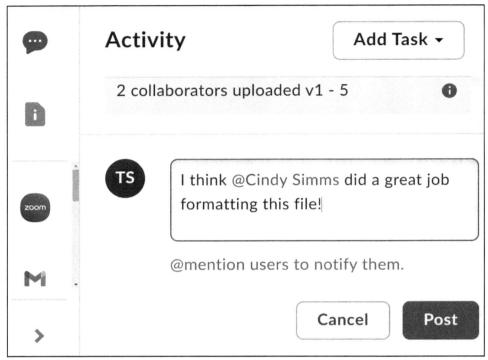

Figure 4.30

Once you type your comment, simply click on the *Post* button to have it attached to that file. Then when you or someone else goes to the preview section of that file, they will be able to see your comment.

If you go back to the comments section and click on the ellipses next to it, you will have the option to edit or delete the comment assuming you are the one who created it.

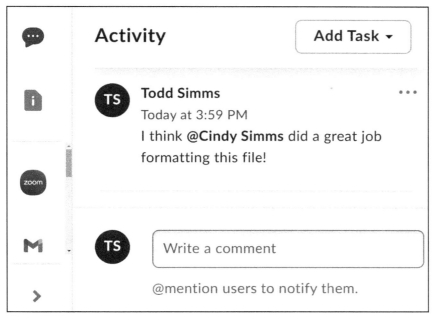

Figure 4.31

When you mention someone in a comment, they will receive an email letting them know about your comment with a button that they can click on to take them directly to your comment in case they wish to reply to it.

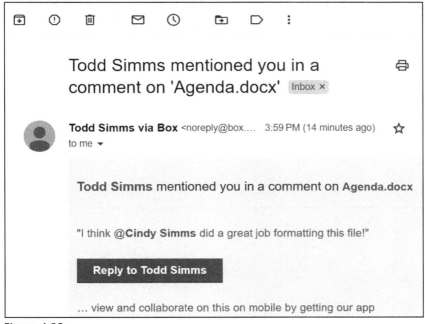

Figure 4.32

You will also be able to see that there is a comment on a file when you look at your file list because it will have a comment bubble icon next to the file name.

Figure 4.33

Tasks

When you are working with other people on projects that require you to share files, you might have the need to assign specific people tasks to make sure that they are doing their part and getting things done on time.

Box will allow you to assign two kinds of tasks to other users based on your needs. You have the option to assign a *general task* which will allow the assignee to mark the task as complete when they are finished. You can also assign an *approval task* where you can assign approvers who will then approve or reject the content assigned to that task.

To assign a task, simply click on a file to open its preview and then from the *Activity* section, click on the *Add Task* button and choose your task type.

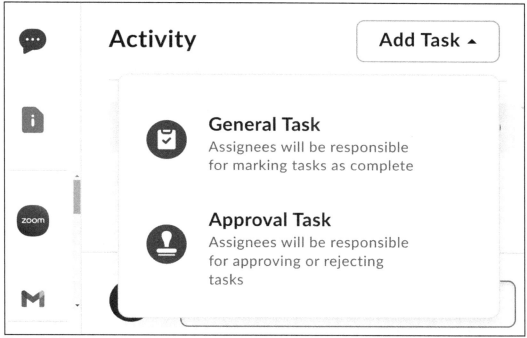

Figure 4.34

When you choose the General Task option, you will need to select the users that you want to assign the task to. Also keep in mind that assignees must be collaborators in the folder containing the file. If you check the box that says *Only one assignee is required to complete this task*, when one of the assignees marks it as complete, then the task itself is completed and the other assignees don't need to also mark it as complete.

You can then add your message describing what needs to be done and also assign a due date if needed.

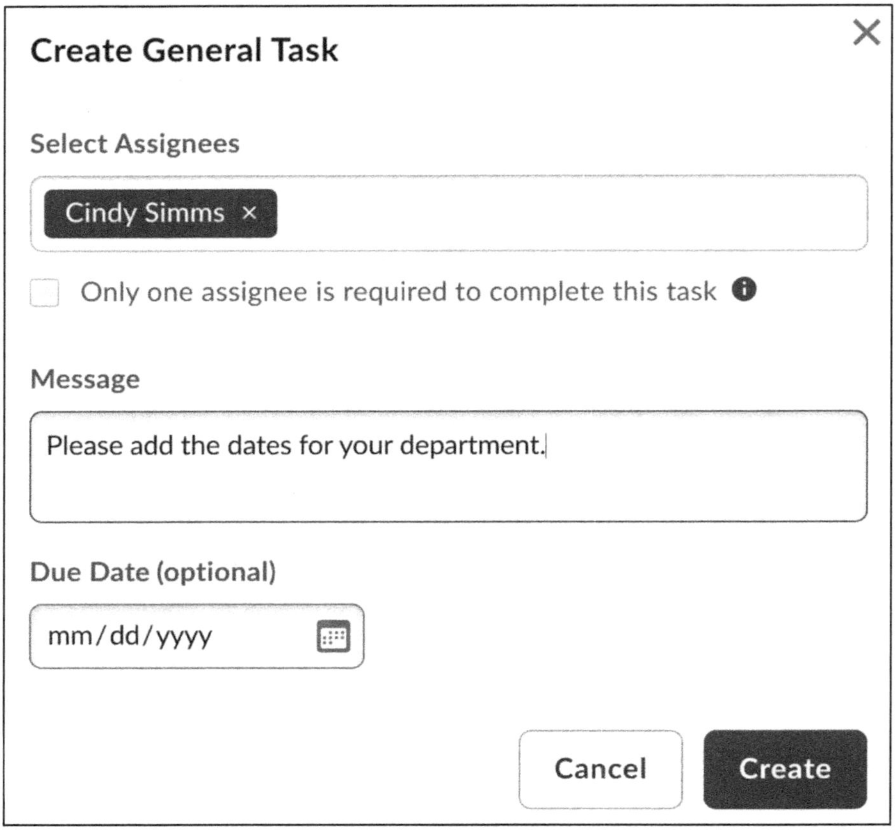

Create General Task   ✕

Select Assignees

Cindy Simms ✕

☐   Only one assignee is required to complete this task ⓘ

Message

Please add the dates for your department.

Due Date (optional)

mm/dd/yyyy   🗓

Cancel   **Create**

Figure 4.35

After you create your task, you and the assignee will then see it in the Activity section when you preview the file.

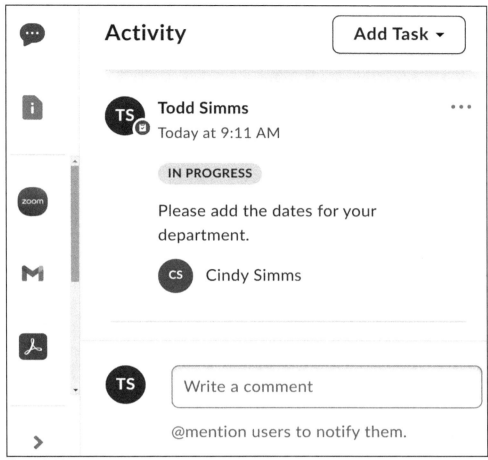

Figure 4.36

The assignee can then click the *Mark as Complete* button when they have finished the work that was required on that file.

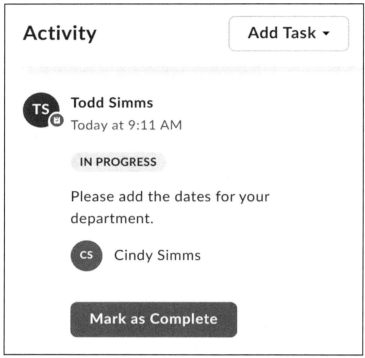

Figure 4.37

Once the task has been marked as complete, you will see the date and time it was completed in your Activity section.

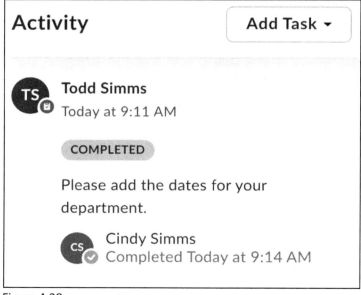

Figure 4.38

You will also see a message in your Notifications area on the main Box screen.

Figure 4.39

Next, I will create an approval task for my calendar file, assign it to two people and set a due date. This time I will not check the box that allows one assignee to be able to mark the task as complete.

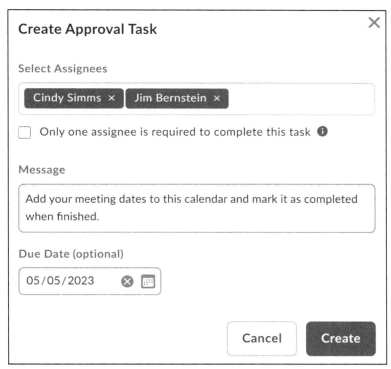

Figure 4.40

After I configure my message and click the *Create* button, each of the assignees will be able to see the task associated with that file in their Box account.

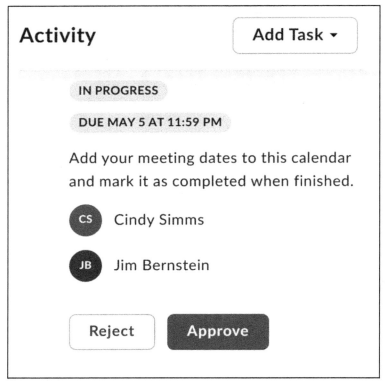

Figure 4.41

If one of the assignees decides to reject the task, then it will show as rejected for all the assignees and also for the person who assigned the task.

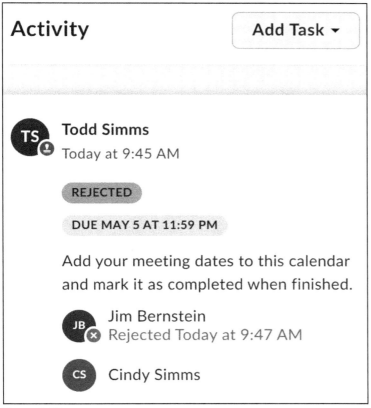

Figure 4.42

If a task is rejected and then another assignee tries to mark it as complete, they will get an error similar to the one shown in figure 4.43 since I unchecked the box that allowed any one assignee the ability to mark a task as complete for everyone.

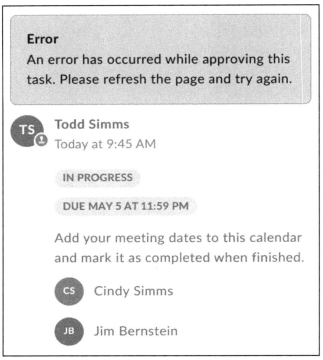

Figure 4.43

The person who assigned the task will also get a notification that the task was rejected.

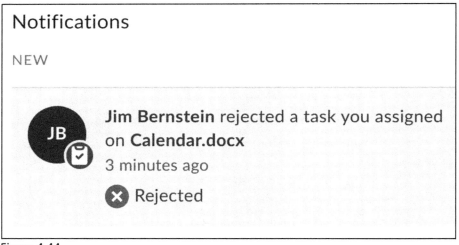

Figure 4.44

I can then reassign the task if I want to make sure everyone approves it and now after both of the assignees mark it as complete, I will see it marked as approved.

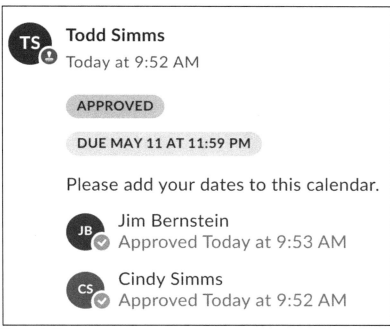

Figure 4.45

Once again, the person who created the task will get a notification that both assignees approved the task.

Figure 4.46

Chapter 5 – Settings and Extras

Now that you hopefully have a thorough understanding of how Box works and how you can use it to backup and share your files and folders, I wanted to spend a little time going over the various Box settings as well as some extra features you might not know that you wanted to know about!

Account Settings

Most apps have various settings and options you can adjust to make the app work more efficiently for you, and Box is no exception. There are quite a few settings you can tinker with and in this section, I will be discussing the settings that I think are the most important to check out.

To get to the Box settings, simply click on your initials in the top right corner and then click on *Account Settings*.

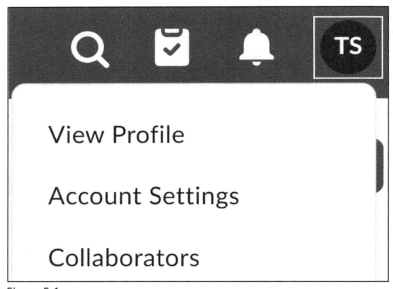

Figure 5.1

Once you are in the Account Settings section, you will notice that there are various categories, each with its own set of options that you can adjust.

Account Settings   Save Changes

Account   Sharing   Notifications Security   Profile   Diagnostics Integrations

Figure 5.2

I will now go over each of these categories and discuss the more important settings.

- **Account** – Here is where you can make adjustments to your account such as viewing your account information, seeing how much storage you have used, and changing your password.

  One area you might want to make some changes to is the default settings section. You might have noticed that when you log into Box, it takes you to the All Files section. If you would like to be taken to a different folder when you log in, you can change that here. You can also change how many files and folders are displayed on a page and whether or not you want your tags to be shown with the file names.

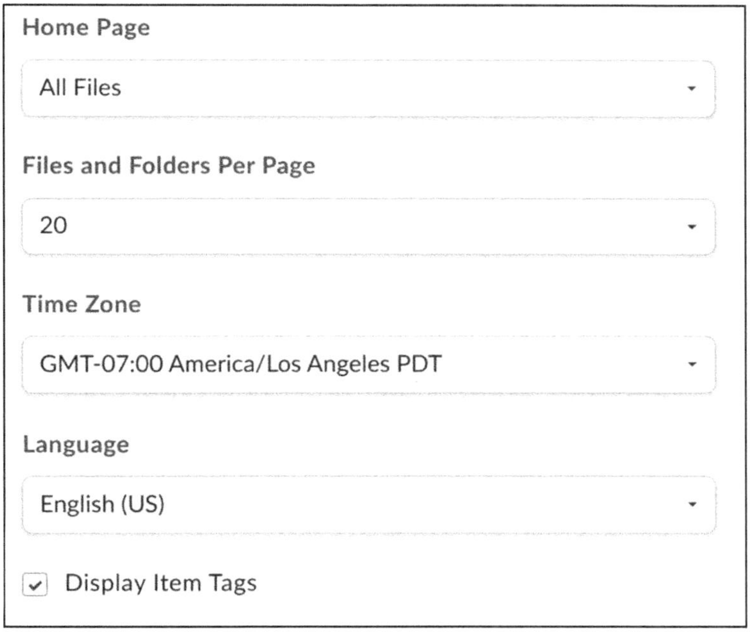

Home Page

All Files

Files and Folders Per Page

20

Time Zone

GMT-07:00 America/Los Angeles PDT

Language

English (US)

☑ Display Item Tags

Figure 5.3

- **Sharing** – Here is where you can change your file and folder sharing defaults. Figure 5.4 shows the default settings and if you hover your mouse over the circle with the **i** inside of it, you will be shown more details about that particular setting.

Allow Shared Links for ⓘ

◉ Folders and files

○ Folders only

○ Files only

○ Nothing, restrict sharing

People who can access shared links

◉ People with the link, people in your company, and people in this folder

○ People in this folder or file only

Default access for new links

◉ People with the link

○ People in this folder or file

Actions link recipients can take ⓘ

◉ Preview, download, and edit the shared item

○ Preview the shared item only

Figure 5.4

- **Notifications –** Having the ability to be notified of certain events is important if you are concerned about things such as meeting deadlines or knowing if someone has edited one of your documents etc.

The notifications settings are broken down into two sections which are for items you own and items you have joined (shared by others). Figure 5.5 shows what types of notifications you can receive and also shows the default settings.

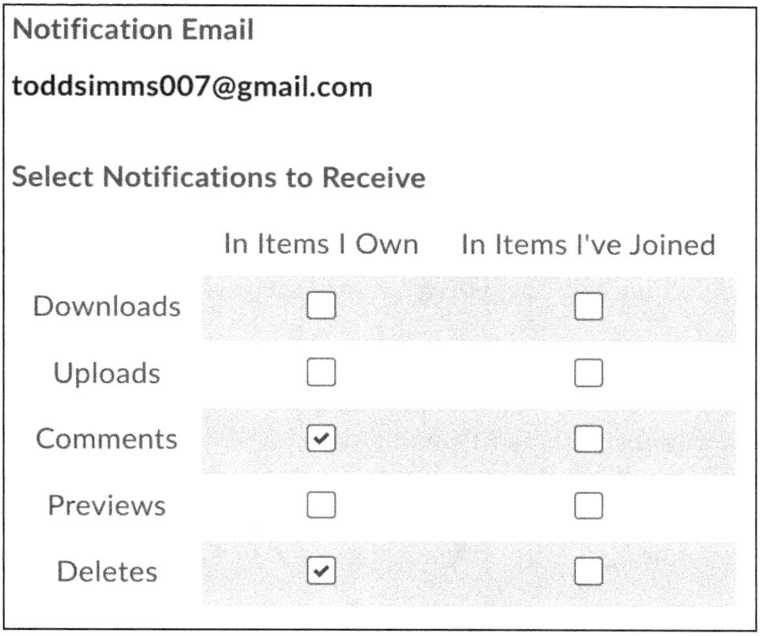

Notification Email

toddsimms007@gmail.com

Select Notifications to Receive

	In Items I Own	In Items I've Joined
Downloads	☐	☐
Uploads	☐	☐
Comments	☑	☐
Previews	☐	☐
Deletes	☑	☐

Figure 5.5

There are also some other settings such as being notified when your account is accessed from a new device and app notifications for Microsoft Teams and Slack.

- **Security** – If you want to check when and where your account was logged in, you can do so from here. If you have a situation where you logged in on a computer that was not yours such as at school and want to have that session forgotten, you can click the X next to that session. You can also click the *Forget All* button to have all of your logged in sessions forgotten.

#	Application	Added	Last Acc...	Last Access Location	Forget App
1	Box Drive	Apr 10, ...	Apr 10, ...	Bellingham, WA, USA	✕
2	Adobe Acrobat for ...	Mar 15, ...	Mar 15, ...	Ashburn, VA, USA	✕
3	Adobe Acrobat for ...	Mar 15, ...	Mar 15, ...	Ashburn, VA, USA	✕
4	Windows Chrome	Mar 14, ...	Apr 10, ...	Bellingham, WA, USA	Current sess...

Forget All

Figure 5.6

- **Profile** – Here you can add a profile picture if you don't want to simply see your initials in the circle at the upper right when you log into your account. You can also change attributes such as your name, company name, website, title, phone and address.

- **Diagnostics** – If you are having problems with your account, you can do things such as test your connection to Box or allow Box support access to your account for 5 days so they can help you troubleshoot any issues you might be having.

- **Integrations** – I had discussed integrations in chapter 3, and these are used to associate third party apps such as Microsoft Word with your Box account. If you need to enable, disable or change any of these integrations, you can do so from here. Figure 5.7 shows how you can set the default apps for Word documents, PowerPoint files, Excel spreadsheets and PDF files.

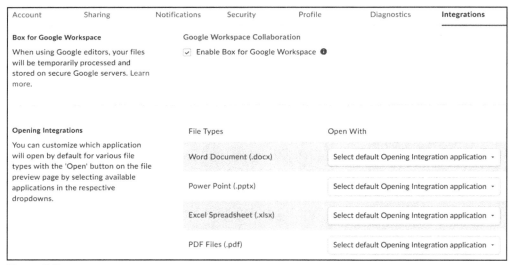

Figure 5.7

Folder Settings

Since folders can store multiple files, it makes sense that there would be some settings related specifically to folders. These settings can be applied to specific folders themselves and are not applied to all folders when you make changes to these settings.

To get to the settings for a folder, simply click on the ellipses next to the folder name and choose *Settings*. The folder settings are broken up into several categories as shown in figures 5.8, 5.9 and 5.10.

The *Collaboration* section will let you determine who can collaborate on the folder and how they can join. The *Shared Link Access* section will let you decide who can access the folder when accessed via a shared link.

Collaboration

Invitation Restrictions

Choose who can collaborate in this folder and how they can join.

☐ Only folder owners and co-owners can send collaborator invites

☐ Restrict collaboration to within Enterprise for Todd Simms

Allow anyone who can access this folder from a shared link to join as a collaborator ⓘ

Allow users to join as: Editor

Shared Link Access

Restrict who can access this folder via shared links.

☑ Only collaborators can access this folder via shared links

For: Files and Folders ▾

| Files and Folders |
| Folders Only |
| Files Only |

Figure 5.8

The *Privacy* settings can be used to hide activity from non-folder owners in case you do not want other people to be able to see who is taking what actions on a folder. If you want to delete or un-share a folder on a certain date without having to remember to do it, you can use the *Automated Actions* settings for this.

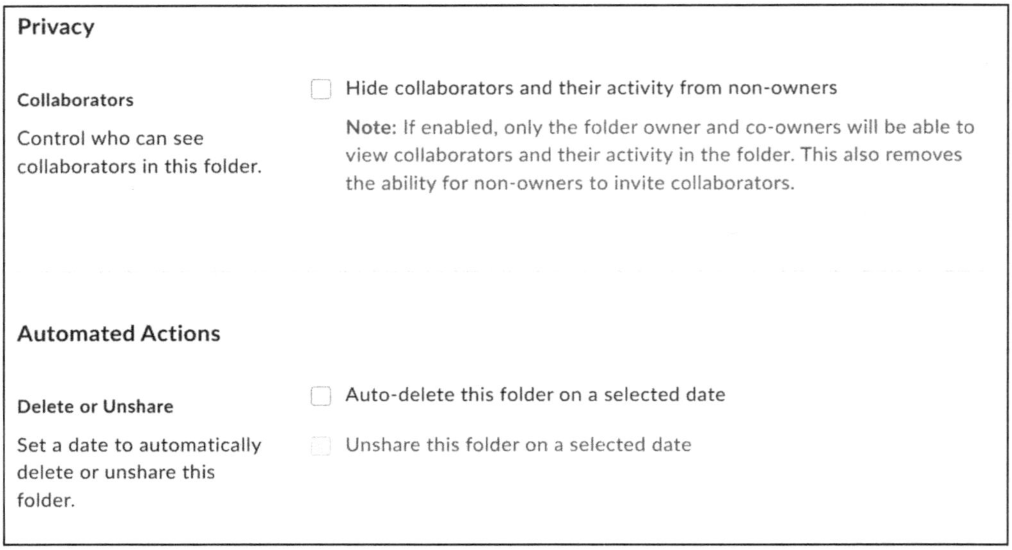

Privacy

Collaborators

Control who can see collaborators in this folder.

☐ Hide collaborators and their activity from non-owners

Note: If enabled, only the folder owner and co-owners will be able to view collaborators and their activity in the folder. This also removes the ability for non-owners to invite collaborators.

Automated Actions

Delete or Unshare

Set a date to automatically delete or unshare this folder.

☐ Auto-delete this folder on a selected date

☐ Unshare this folder on a selected date

Figure 5.9

Just like you saw in the main Box settings, you can also set notification options for folders themselves as seen in figure 5.10.

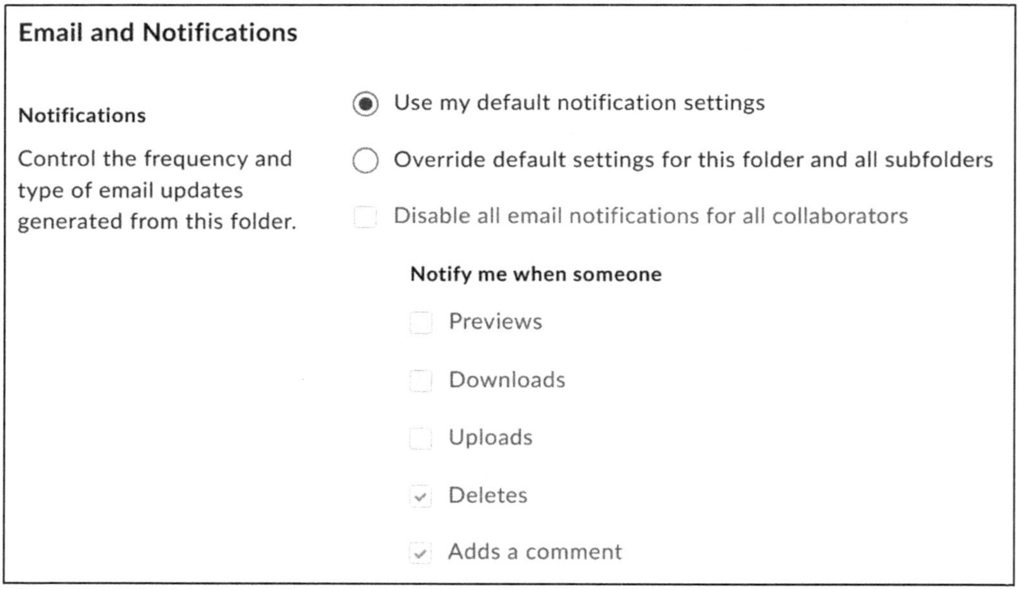

Email and Notifications

Notifications

Control the frequency and type of email updates generated from this folder.

◉ Use my default notification settings

◯ Override default settings for this folder and all subfolders

☐ Disable all email notifications for all collaborators

Notify me when someone

☐ Previews

☐ Downloads

☐ Uploads

☑ Deletes

☑ Adds a comment

Figure 5.10

Box Admin Console

If you decide to go with one of the business plans for your Box account, you will then have access to the Box Admin Console where you can perform more advanced account management tasks. The Admin Console is used to manage settings for your organization and its users. This way, you can adjust settings and have them apply to everyone who is a part of your Box environment. I will go over the basic sections of the Admin Console so you can get an idea of what you can do with it in case you decide to upgrade to a business account.

Figure 5.11 shows how the Admin Console looks and you can see there are many different categories on the left that you can access to configure settings.

Figure 5.11

Figures 5.12 and 5.13 show how you can manage users that are part of your organization.

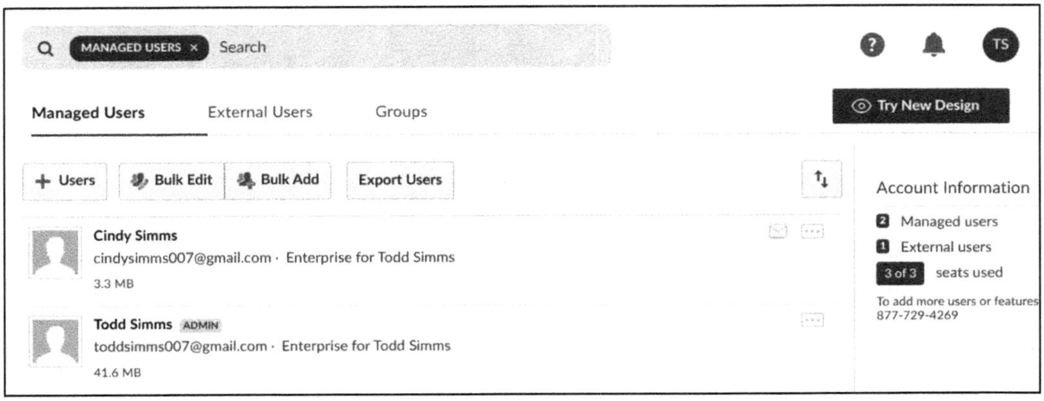

Figure 5.12

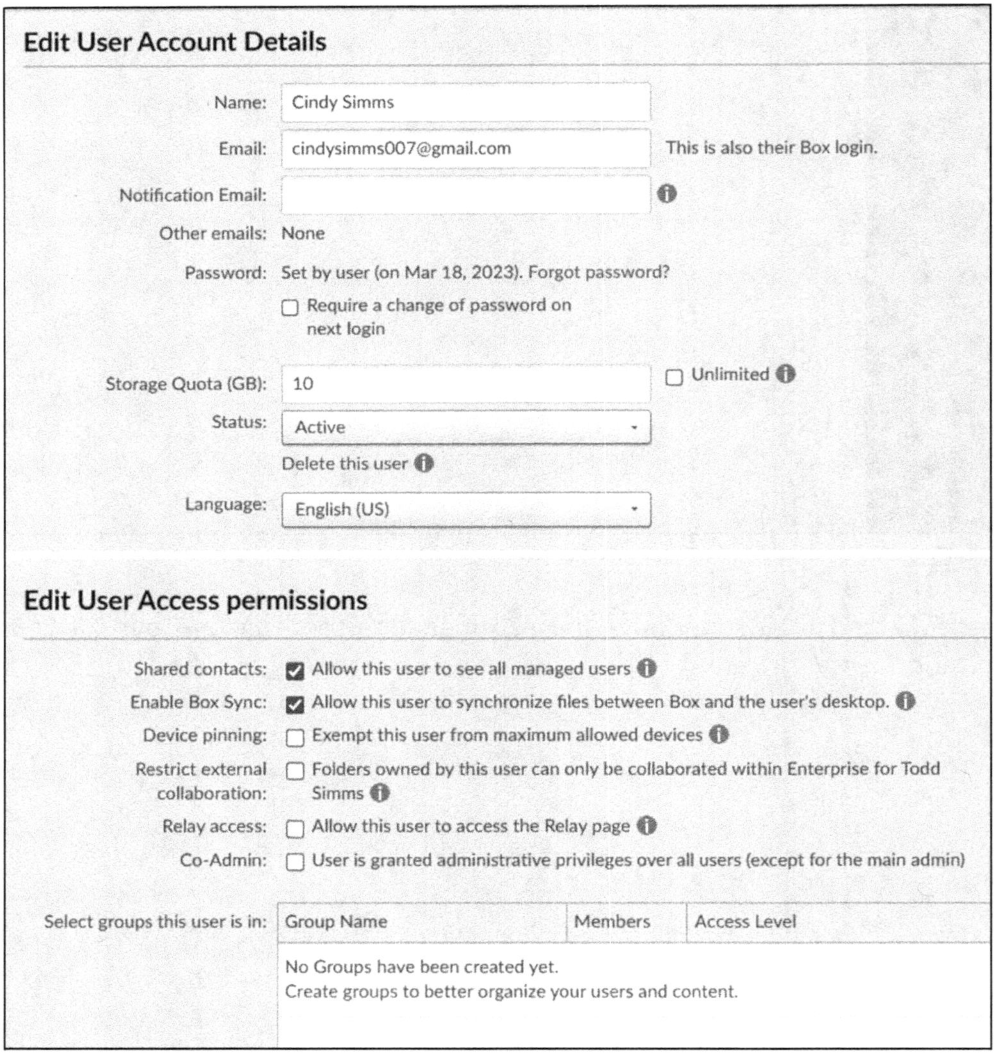

Figure 5.13

Figure 5.14 shows that you can also manage users who are not part of your organization but are collaborating on your files or folders. You will not have the same configuration options for external users as you do for managed (internal) users.

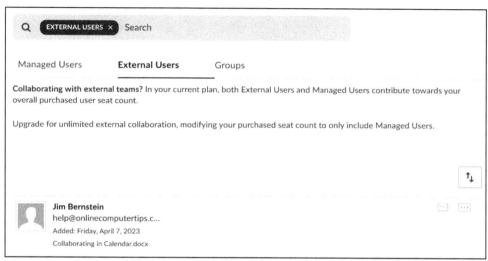

Figure 5.14

The Admin Console will also allow you to enable or disable apps and integrations for all users in your organization from one central location.

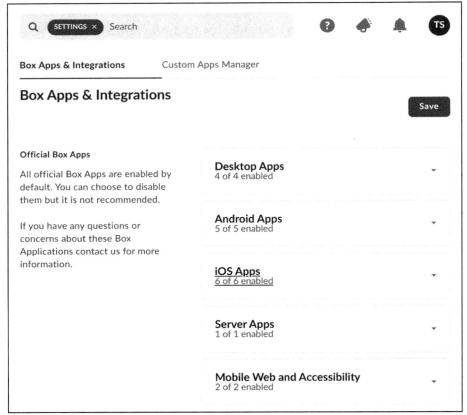

Figure 5.15

At the bottom, you will find a link to take you to the enterprise settings where you can fine tune how your Box organization and its users function.

Figure 5.16

Box Notes

If you want an easy way to create quick notes and basic documents that you can then easily share with others, you might want to give Box Notes a try. Notes is built into your Box account and can be accessed by clicking on the Notes section in the navigation area on the left side of the screen.

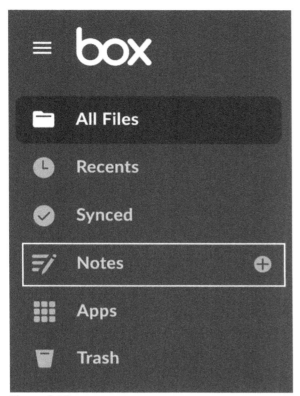

Figure 5.17

The first time you click on Notes, you may be asked for a default save location for your notes. Here you can choose an existing folder or create a new one just for your notes.

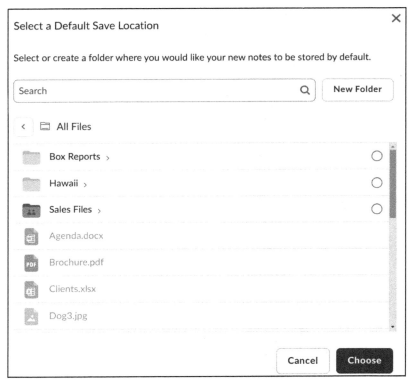

Figure 5.18

For my notes, I will create a new folder called *My Notes*.

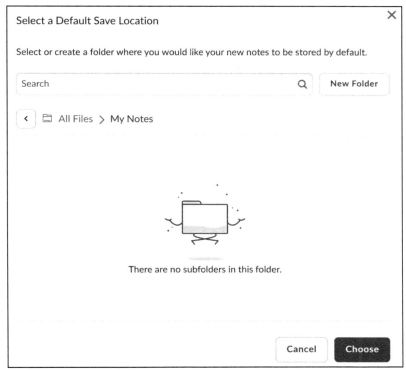

Figure 5.19

Now when I create a new note, it will be named *Untiled Note* with the date it was created.

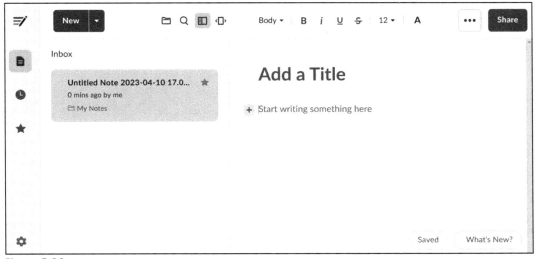

Figure 5.20

Once you add a title to the note, it will then change the name of the note to match the title.

Figure 5.21

Now I will add some basic information to my new note. I can either start by typing in some text or I can click on the + sign to choose items such as a table, divider line, call out, table of contents, code block or block quote.

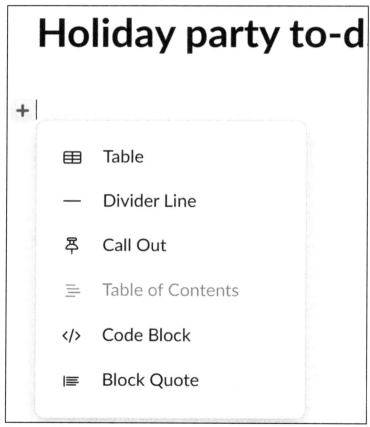

Figure 5.22

At the top of the screen, you will have some basic text editing options such as bold, italics, underline and strikethrough. You can also change the font size and color as well as add various types of lists such as a numbered list. The up-arrow icon is used to insert an image from your computer or a Box shared link. The last icon in figure 5.23 is used to insert a table into your note.

Figure 5.23

I decided to add a bulleted list to my note and then added a picture of what the party invitation might look like.

Figure 5.24

The icons at the upper left of the screen are used to open existing notes, search all your notes by title or contents, show or hide the sidebar and have your note take up the full width of the screen.

Figure 5.25

The icons at the upper right can be used to add and view comments related to your notes or share your notes with other Box users just like you would any other type of file.

Figure 5.26

Clicking on the ellipses next to the comment button will give you other options such as deleting, moving, copying or printing your note. You can even save a note as a template so you can use its configuration again for a different note.

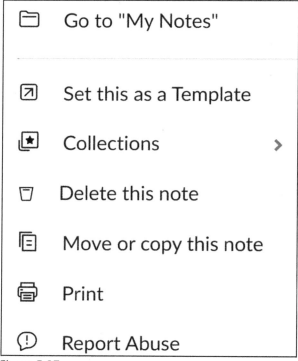

Figure 5.27

At the left side of the Notes interface, you will have your Inbox which will show you a listing of your notes, then under that you will have a section where you can view your most recent notes. The star icon is used as a place to view your favorite notes. You can mark a note as a favorite by clicking the star icon next to its name as seen in figure 5.28 for the Meeting notes example.

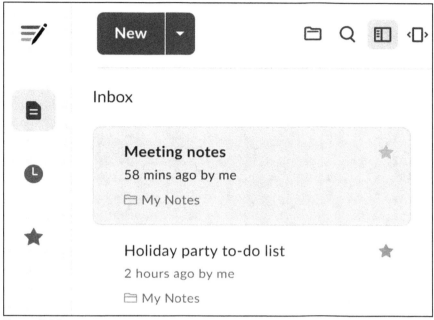

Figure 5.28

At the bottom left corner of the screen, you will have a gear icon (figure 5.29) that will allow you to configure some basic settings such as changing the default save location of your notes or viewing the Notes keyboard and emoji shortcuts (figure 5.30).

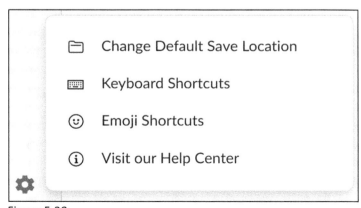

Figure 5.29

Keyboard Shortcuts		Emoji Shortcuts	
Ctrl + <	Decrease font size	(c)	©
Ctrl + >	Increase font size	<3	♥
Ctrl + E	Center text	/shrug	¯_(ツ)_/¯
Ctrl + J	Left align text	:)	☺
Ctrl + ⇧ + X	Check/uncheck checklist item	:P	😝
Ctrl + ⇧ + O	Show/hide comments	;)	😉
Ctrl + ⇧ + F	Toggle search	<<	«
Ctrl + ⇧ + U	Show/hide sidebar	>>	»
Ctrl + ⇧ + 1	View recent notes	<-	←
Ctrl + ⇧ + 2	View favorites	1*2	1×2
Ctrl + ⇧ + 6	Toggle checklist	!=	≠
Ctrl + ⇧ + 7	Toggle numbered list	1/2	½
Ctrl + ⇧ + 8	Toggle bulleted list	+/-	±
Ctrl + ⇧ + 9	Strikethrough	(r)	®
Ctrl + Alt + N	Create note	->	→
Ctrl + ⇧ + A	Add annotation		
Ctrl + K	Add hyperlink		
Ctrl + Z	Undo		
Ctrl + /	Toggle key shortcut legend		

Figure 5.30

Embedding Widgets

If you have your own website or maybe a blog that you maintain, you might want to share your photos or other files on that site so that other people can view them directly from your website itself without needing to have a Box account or have the folder be shared with them.

This can be done by embedding a folder widget onto your website that links directly to that folder in Box. The first thing you will need to do is select that folder, click on the ellipses and then choose *More Actions > Embed Widget*. You will then be given the embed code that you will use on your website and have a choice as to what size the widget will be and how you want your files sorted and displayed.

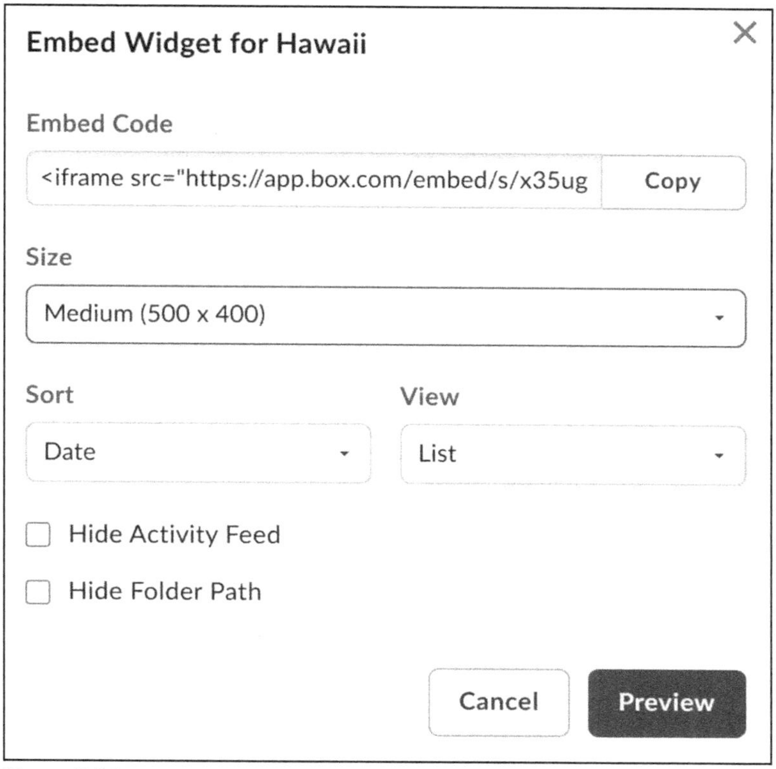

Embed Widget for Hawaii   ✕

Embed Code

| `<iframe src="https://app.box.com/embed/s/x35ug` | Copy |

Size

| Medium (500 x 400) | ▾ |

Sort   View

| Date | ▾ | | List | ▾ |

☐ Hide Activity Feed

☐ Hide Folder Path

Cancel   **Preview**

Figure 5.31

The process for adding the embed code to your website will vary based on what you are using for your site but once you have it ready to go, it will look similar to figure 5.32. You will notice that the first thing visitors will need to do before seeing your files is to drag the white cloud into the dark cloud to prove that you are a real person and not some kind of bot trying to get into the shared folder.

Figure 5.32

If you view the widget while logged into your Box account, you will have the option to do things such as search, add a quick note, and upload additional files and folders.

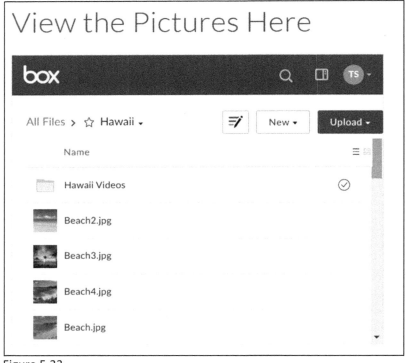

Figure 5.33

If you are not logged in, you will only be able to view and download the files from the folder.

Figure 5.34

When you click on a file, you will then be shown that file within the widget assuming it's a type of file that can be viewed online without being downloaded first, just like you encounter when opening files from Box itself.

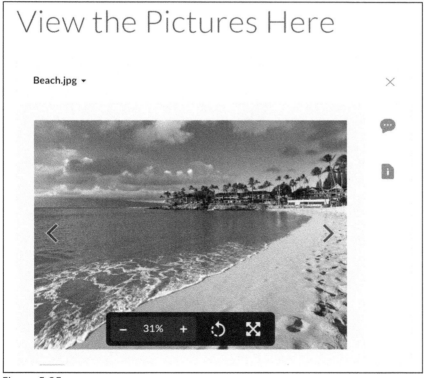

Figure 5.35

Apps

You might have noticed that you have the capability to do things such as open your files with Microsoft Office apps or open PDF files with Adobe Acrobat and assumed that these features just came included with Box itself. But in reality, the reason you can perform these tasks is because Box allows you to install third party apps to improve the functionality of Box itself.

You might have noticed over on the left in the navigation area that you have a section called Apps (figure 5.36). Once you go to the Apps section, you will see various categories as well as featured apps. Anything with a checkmark next to it means that it is already installed in your account. You can click on any one of the apps to see more information about that app.

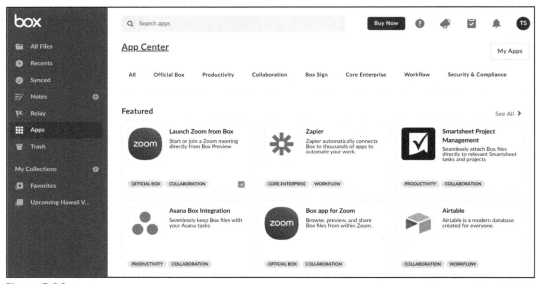

Figure 5.36

If you click on the *My Apps* button, you will see which apps you have installed in your environment.

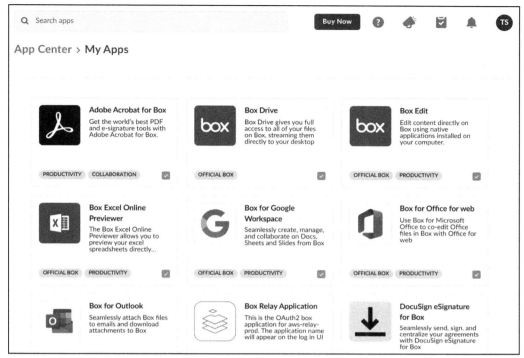

Figure 5.37

You can then click on an app to view its details, share a link to that app or remove it if it's no longer needed.

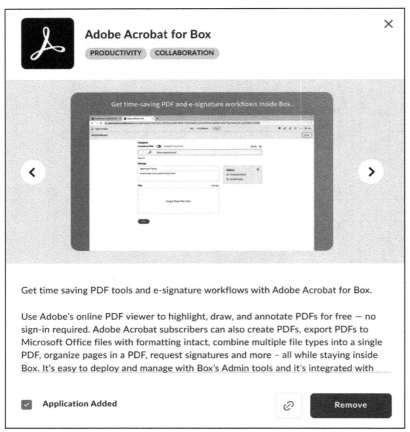

Figure 5.38

If you want to see what other apps are available, you can do a search from the search box at the top of the screen. Figure 5.39 shows some of the results when I search for PDF.

One thing you will notice when trying to add apps is that many of them are for mobile devices such as iPhones, iPads and Android devices. You will also notice that you will be taken to external websites where you will need to do some additional configuration to get these apps to work with Box and it's not a straightforward process like it is when you install an app on your phone.

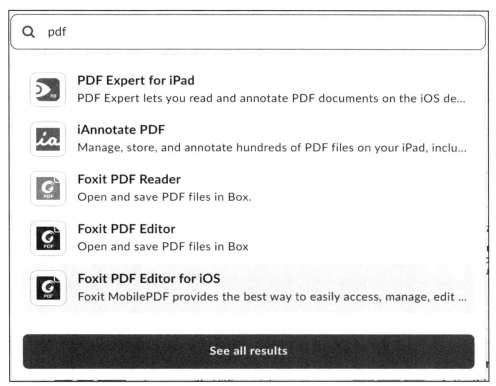

Figure 5.39

If I search for Box to find apps specific to Box itself, I will see many of the apps that I already have installed.

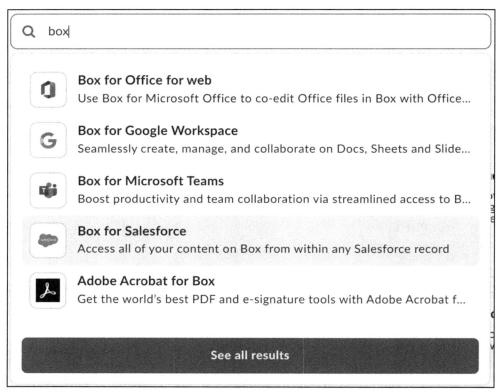

Figure 5.40

If I then try to install Box for Microsoft Teams for example, I will be shown the details for that app and can then click the *Add* button to install it for my account.

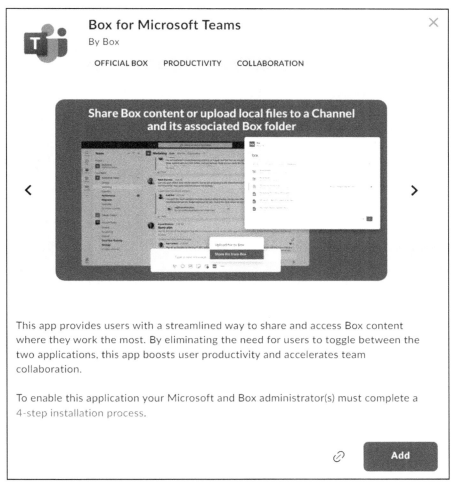

Figure 5.41

You will then be shown what permissions the app will need with your account so make sure you are ok with this before clicking on the *Proceed* button.

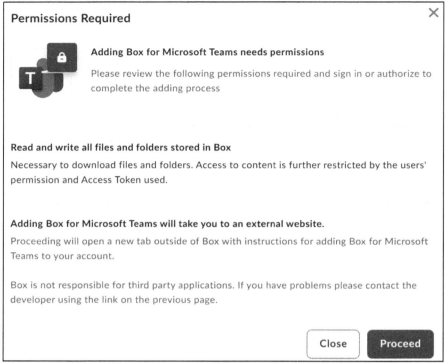

Figure 5.42

Once I click on the Proceed button, I am taken to an external website which is common for most apps. I am then told that it is a 4 step process to install the app and will need to make sure I have the ability to do so (figure 4.3). For this app, I will need to have access to the Box Admin Console and if you don't have the business plan, you will not be able to accomplish this. This is an example of how tricky installing Box apps can be so if you are having issues getting them configured, you are not alone!

You can enable Box for Teams for your entire organization via your Box Admin Console and you can pre-pin the Box app in Teams for your entire organization in the Microsoft Teams admin center. Also, when you install this integration, Box provides you with several security settings that control how Box for Teams behaves, which significantly reduces the amount of manual work required to get started.

Broadly, there are 4 procedures to follow when you deploy the Box for Teams integration in your enterprise:

1. Give API Consent for Box and Microsoft to share data

2. Configure Microsoft 365 Permissions

3. Authorize Microsoft in the Box Admin Console

4. (a) Add the Box application to your Teams, and/or (b) Pre-pin the Box application in Teams

You must complete all 4 procedures.

Figure 5.43

Box Sign

It's very common these days to have documents signed electronically so you don't have to mail a copy for the other party to sign and then send it back to you while you wait.

There are many electronic signature services that you can use for this purpose but if you are a Box user, you can do so for free right from Box itself. Box allows you to define up to 35 recipients per signature request. If you are using the free Box account, you can have up to 5 documents signed electronically per month.

To start the signature process, simply go to the Box Sign section in the left side navigation panel. If you are trying out a higher version of Box as a demo, then you might not have the Sign option until you choose your plan.

Once you are in the Sign section, you can then either request a signature or sign a document yourself to then be sent out to others. For my example, I am going to request a signature on a contract document.

Figure 5.44

Once I choose the Request Signature option, I can then upload the document to be signed from my computer or choose it from a folder in my Box account. At the right side of the screen, you will have several options for fields that can be added to the document such as signature, date, initials, checkbox and so on. I will just be adding the Signature field to my document.

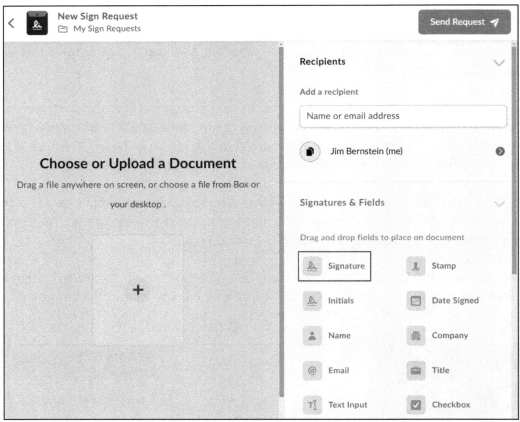

Figure 5.45

Once I open my document, I can then drag and drop the signature field to the location on the document where I want the other person or people to sign (figure 5.46).

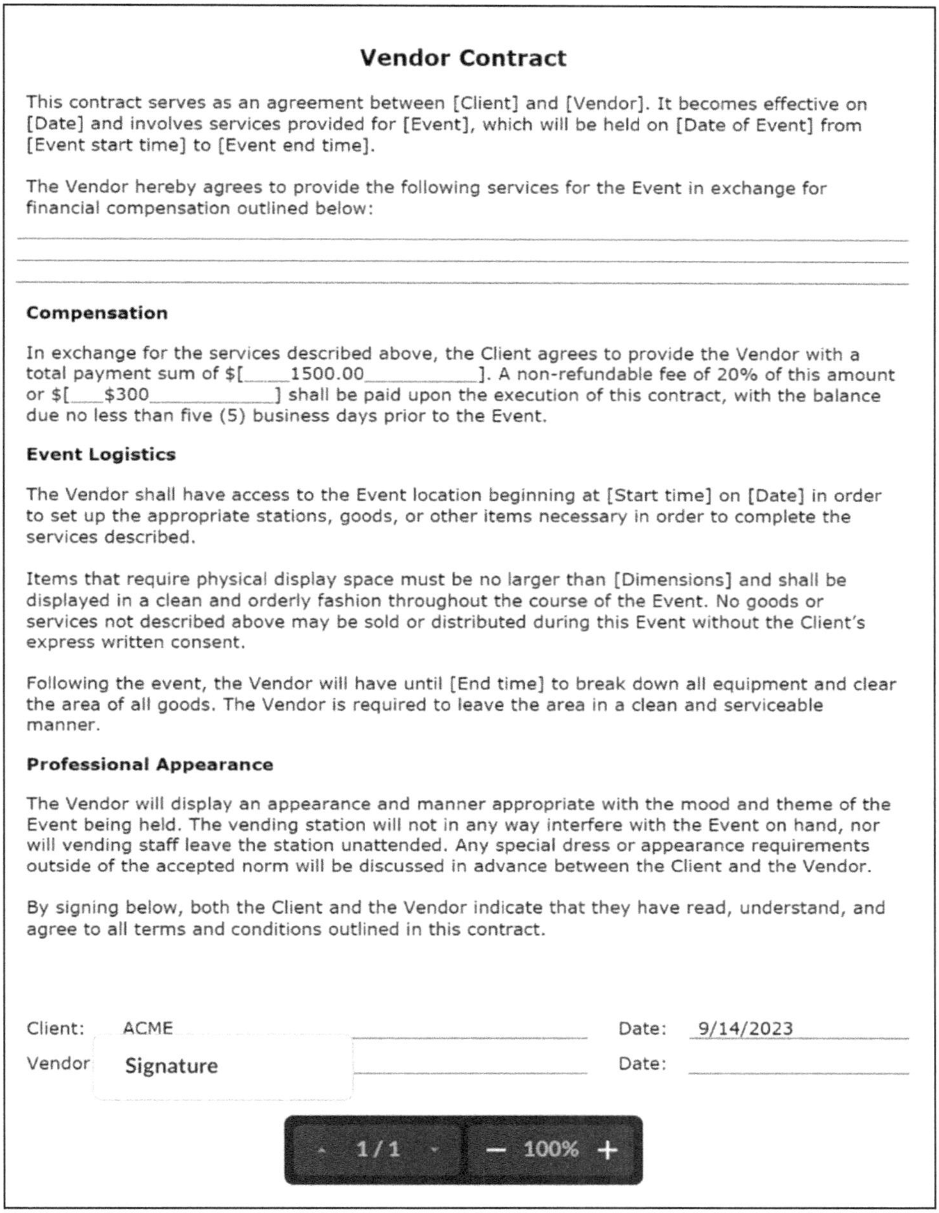

Vendor Contract

This contract serves as an agreement between [Client] and [Vendor]. It becomes effective on [Date] and involves services provided for [Event], which will be held on [Date of Event] from [Event start time] to [Event end time].

The Vendor hereby agrees to provide the following services for the Event in exchange for financial compensation outlined below:

_____

_____
_____

Compensation

In exchange for the services described above, the Client agrees to provide the Vendor with a total payment sum of $[_____1500.00_____]. A non-refundable fee of 20% of this amount or $[___$300_____] shall be paid upon the execution of this contract, with the balance due no less than five (5) business days prior to the Event.

Event Logistics

The Vendor shall have access to the Event location beginning at [Start time] on [Date] in order to set up the appropriate stations, goods, or other items necessary in order to complete the services described.

Items that require physical display space must be no larger than [Dimensions] and shall be displayed in a clean and orderly fashion throughout the course of the Event. No goods or services not described above may be sold or distributed during this Event without the Client's express written consent.

Following the event, the Vendor will have until [End time] to break down all equipment and clear the area of all goods. The Vendor is required to leave the area in a clean and serviceable manner.

Professional Appearance

The Vendor will display an appearance and manner appropriate with the mood and theme of the Event being held. The vending station will not in any way interfere with the Event on hand, nor will vending staff leave the station unattended. Any special dress or appearance requirements outside of the accepted norm will be discussed in advance between the Client and the Vendor.

By signing below, both the Client and the Vendor indicate that they have read, understand, and agree to all terms and conditions outlined in this contract.

Client: ACME _____   _____   Date: 9/14/2023 _____

Vendor   Signature _____   _____   Date: _____

▲ 1 / 1 ▾   — 100% +

Figure 5.46

I will then need to click on the signature field and then select a recipient to assign the signature to.

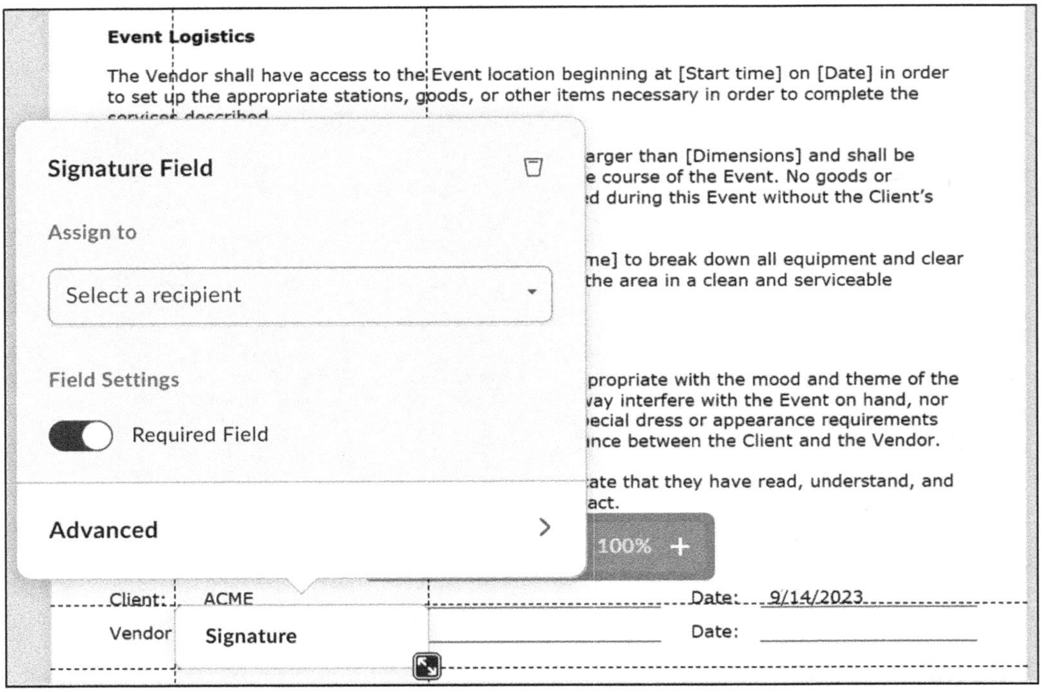

Event Logistics

The Vendor shall have access to the Event location beginning at [Start time] on [Date] in order to set up the appropriate stations, goods, or other items necessary in order to complete the

Signature Field

Assign to

Select a recipient

Field Settings

Required Field

Advanced

arger than [Dimensions] and shall be
e course of the Event. No goods or
d during this Event without the Client's

ne] to break down all equipment and clear
the area in a clean and serviceable

propriate with the mood and theme of the
vay interfere with the Event on hand, nor
ecial dress or appearance requirements
nce between the Client and the Vendor.

ate that they have read, understand, and
act.

100% +

Client: ACME   Date: 9/14/2023

Vendor Signature   Date:

Figure 5.47

At the right side of the screen under the field options, you will have settings for email notifications, file expiration and where you would like to have your signed documents saved in your Box account (figure 5.48). The default is the *My Signed Requests* folder. I will add the recipient's email address and a message requesting a signature in the Email Notifications section.

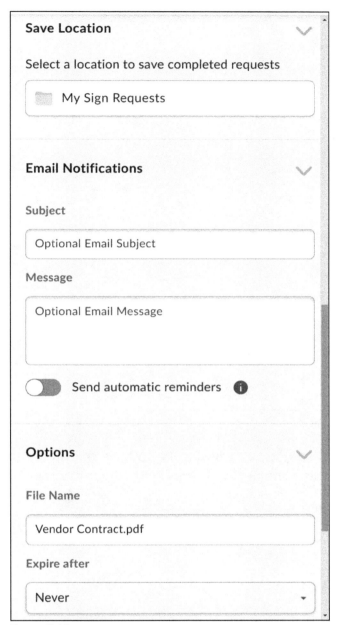

Figure 5.48

Once you add a recipient to your signature field, you can then click on their name at the upper right of the screen to modify their role if you want to change them from a signer to an approver.

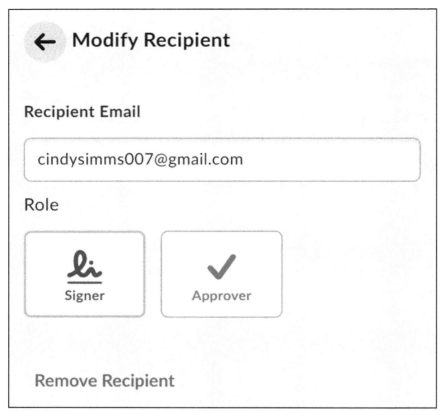

Figure 5.49

When I click on the sender's name, you can see that I also have the option to choose the *Get a copy* role. For this example, I will be using the *Approver* role for the sender.

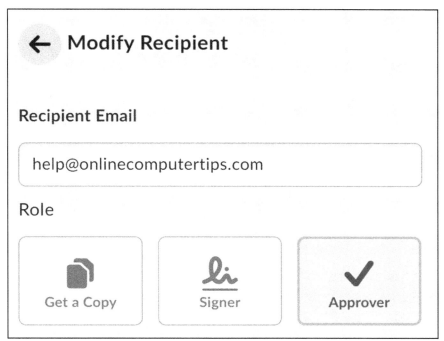

Figure 5.50

Once you have the recipients assigned to the signature task, you can then specify a signing order if needed before clicking the *Send Request* box. Since I only have one person that will be signing my document, I will not choose this option.

Send Request ✈

Recipients ⌄

Add a recipient

> Name or email address

✓ Jim Bernstein (me)   `1` ❯

✍ cindysimms007@gmail.com   `2` ❯

⬤ Specify Signing Order

Figure 5.51

Since I made myself an approver, I will then be prompted to agree to the Box electronic record and signature disclosure, the terms of service and the privacy policy. If my role was set to Get a copy, I would not be presented with this agreement prompt. You can read over each one of these by clicking the link for any one of them. If I agree to the terms, I can then click the *Accept & Continue* button.

‹ ✍ **Vendor Contract.pdf**
Powered by Box Sign

☑ **By checking this box you:**

  • Agree to use electronic records and signatures and confirm you have read the <u>Electronic Record and Signature Disclosure</u>

  • Agree to Box's <u>Terms of Service</u> and confirm you have read Box's <u>Privacy Policy</u>

Accept & Continue

Figure 5.52

I can then view the signature request details and then be able to decline, reassign, download or print it as well as have the option to report abuse. I also have the option to approve it but will wait until I get my signature back before doing so.

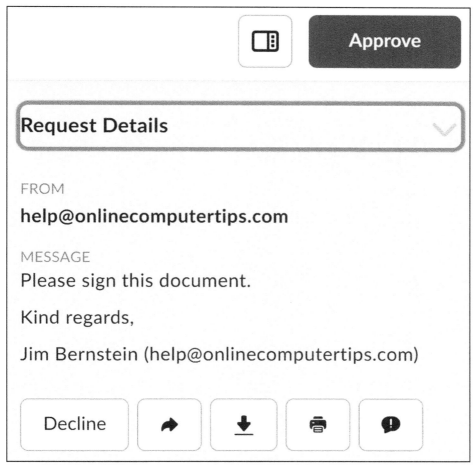

Figure 5.53

Now when I go back to the Sign section in Box, I will see my new signature request showing as in progress.

Figure 5.54

If I were to click on this request, I would see its details showing me that it has been sent and is waiting for a signature.

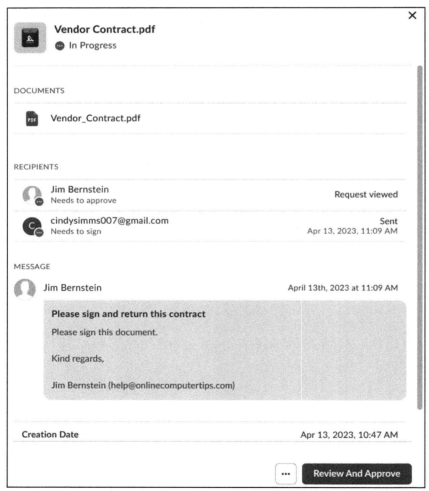

Figure 5.55

The recipient of the signature request will also get an email asking them to review and sign my document.

Figure 5.56

Then will then have to accept the same Box terms that I will when I approve the signature.

Figure 5.57

To start the signing process, they will need to click on the *Begin* button at the upper right of the screen.

Figure 5.58

They can then click on the signature box to start the signing process.

Professional Appearance

The Vendor will display an appearance and manner appropriate with the m
Event being held. The vending station will not in any way interfere with the
will vending staff leave the station unattended. Any special dress or appea
outside of the accepted norm will be discussed in advance between the Cli

By signing below, both the Client and the Vendor indicate that they have r
agree to all terms and conditions outlined in this contract.

Client: _____ACME_____   Date: _

Vendor _____   Date: _

Signature

Place Signature here

Figure 5.59

To sign the document, they can either draw or type in their signature. If they have
an image of their signature, they can upload that as well or even choose from a
saved signature. I will choose the *type* option for my example.

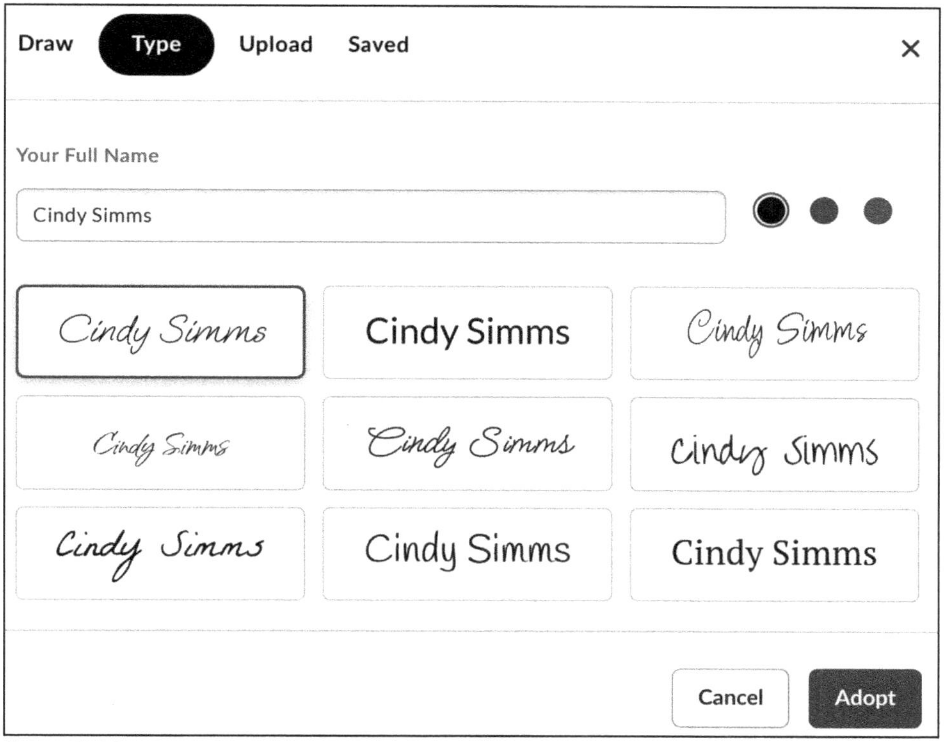

Figure 5.60

Figure 5.61 shows their signature and if everything looks good, they can click on the *Sign & Finish* button.

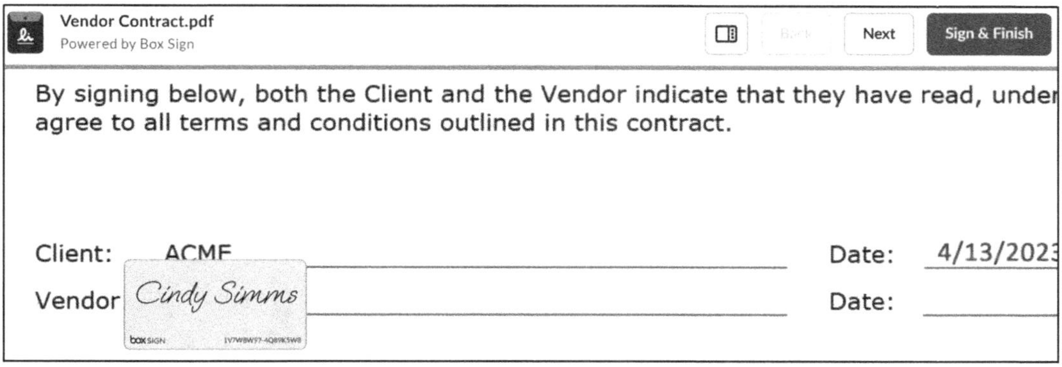

Figure 5.61

If the signee checks the details of the request, they will have the same options to decline or forward the request and so on.

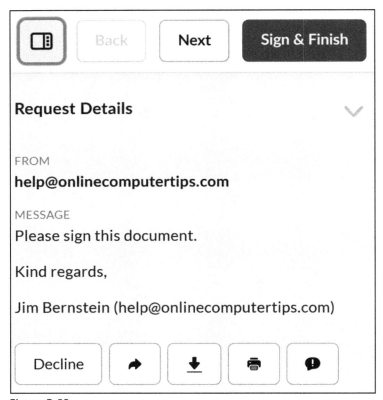

Figure 5.62

After clicking Sign & Finish, they will be shown a screen letting them know the process is complete.

Figure 5.63

I will then receive an email from Box letting me know that the document has been signed.

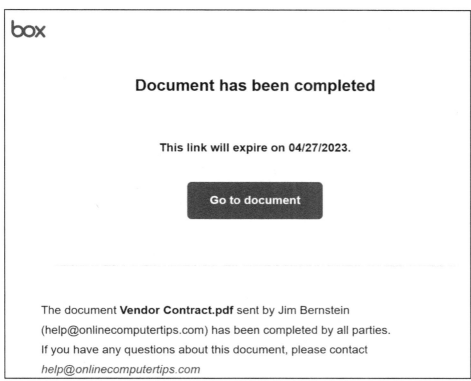

box

Document has been completed

This link will expire on 04/27/2023.

Go to document

The document **Vendor Contract.pdf** sent by Jim Bernstein
(help@onlinecomputertips.com) has been completed by all parties.
If you have any questions about this document, please contact
help@onlinecomputertips.com

Figure 5.64

Now when I go back to the request details, I will see that Cindy has signed the document and I can then review and approve the signature request to complete the process.

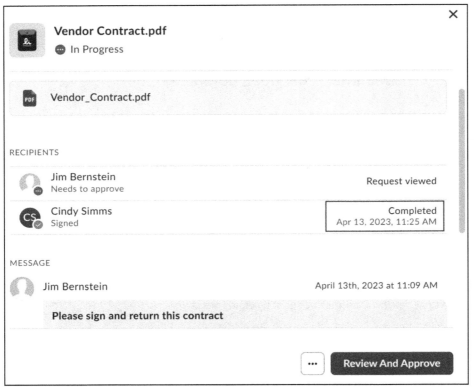

Figure 5.65

Once I approve the signature request and go back to the details, I can see that it is marked as signed.

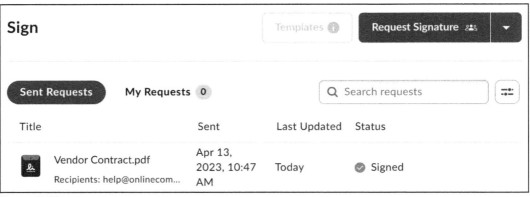

Figure 5.66

If I were to then go to the folder that contains my signed documents, I would see might signed vendor contract file as well as a log file showing the details about the signing process (figure 5.68).

Figure 5.67

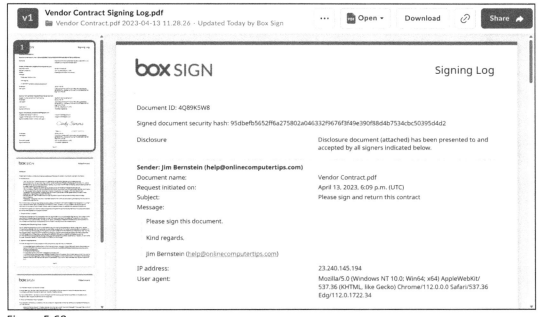

Figure 5.68

Box File Requests

If you are working with other people and need them to send you some files, then you can use the Box File Request feature which will allow them to upload files directly to a folder in your Box account. This way you do not need to worry about receiving multiple emails with large attachments to get the files you need. And if the people who you need the files from do not have a Box account, they can still upload files without having to create one.

The file request feature comes with the Business account type so if you are using the free or one of the lower-level plans, you will not have this option.

To start the process, open the folder you want to use for your file requests or create a new one if you want to keep things separate. I will make a new folder called *Construction Project Files* and then open it to see the *File Request* section under the Sharing details.

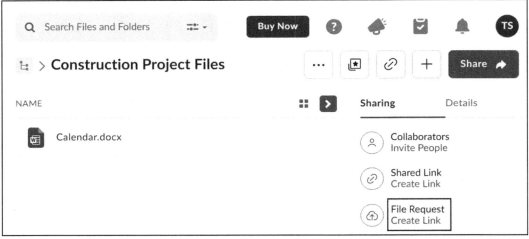

Figure 5.69

Once I click on *Create Link*, I will have the option to copy the link that I can then send to the people whom I need the files from.

File Request ✕

Share this link to a webpage so others can upload files to this folder.

⬤◯ Link is enabled   Settings

https://app.box.com/f/3b79de52a70146e5894f0f   Copy   </>

🌐 This webpage is publicly available to anyone with the link.

Preview   **Edit**

Figure 5.70

If I click on the *Edit* button, I can customize my request form by changing the name from the default *Submit files*.

167

Figure 5.71

If I click on the *Add a field* button, I can then add a box for them to enter their email address and also a description for the file upload.

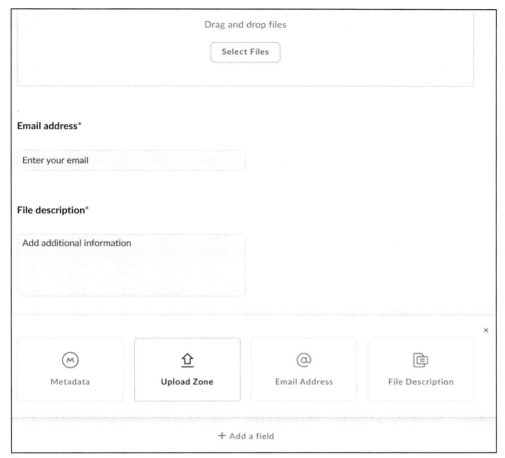

Figure 5.72

Clicking on the ellipses will give me the option to make these fields required if that is what I want to do.

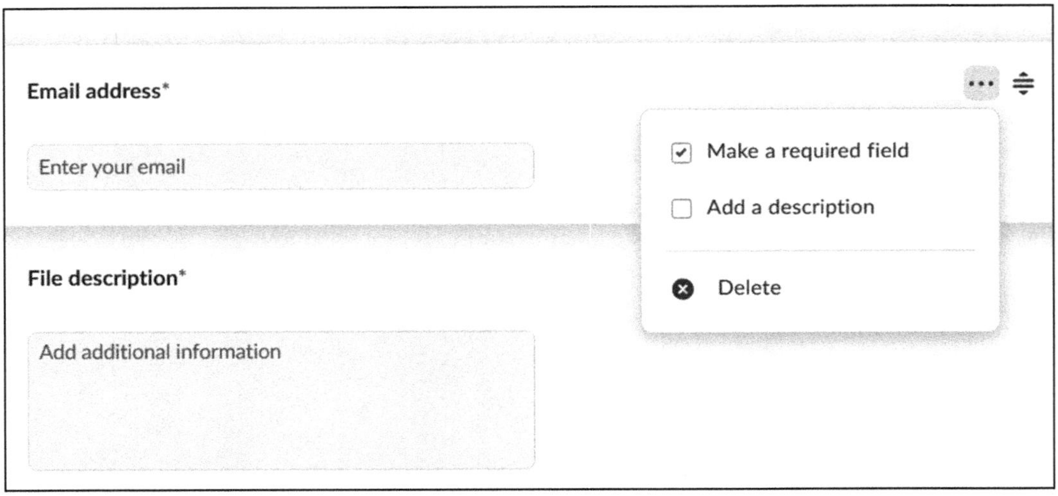

Figure 5.73

I can then click the *Theme* button to change the color of the request form or add a custom logo to the top of it.

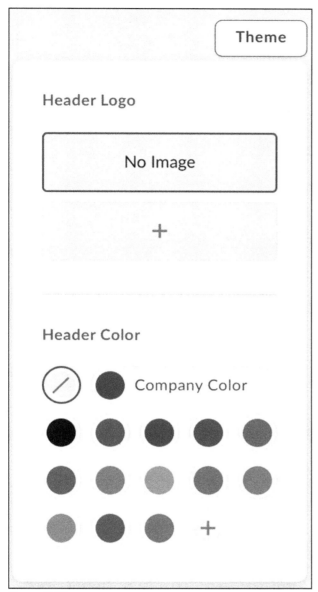

Figure 5.74

Finally, I will click on the *Save* button and then the *Share* button to copy the link that now has my changes. Then I can paste it into an email or instant message and send it to those who I want to have upload files to my folder.

When the recipient receives the email, it will look similar to figure 5.75.

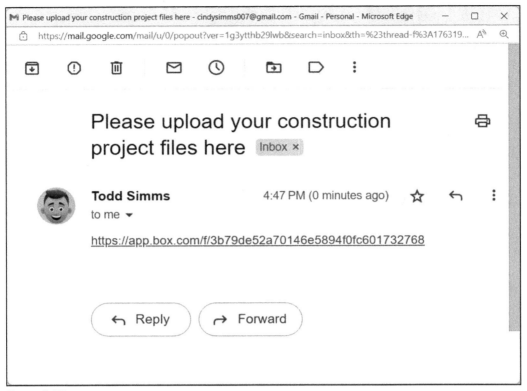

Figure 5.75

When they click the link, they will be taken to my upload form where they can drag and drop their files and type in their email address. They can also add a note if they like.

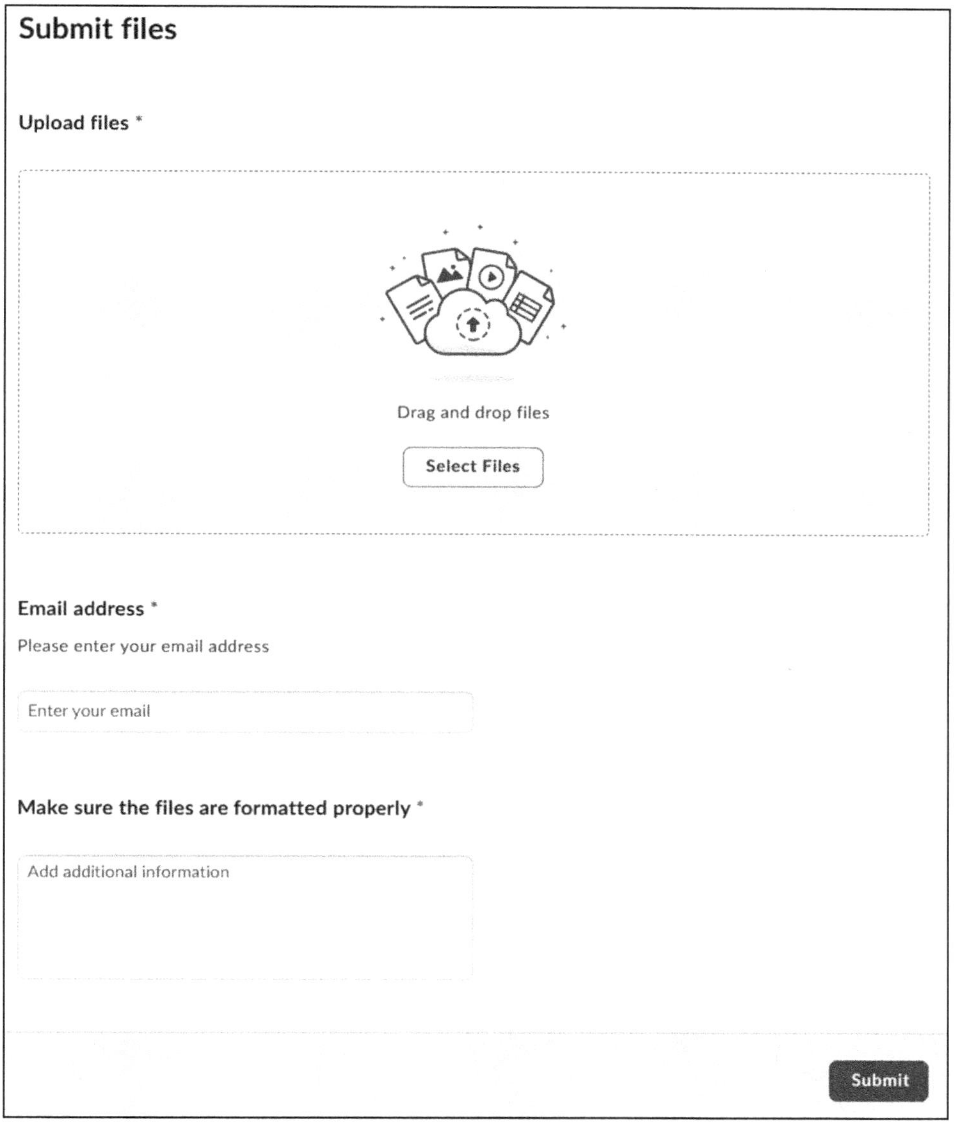

Submit files

Upload files *

Drag and drop files

Select Files

Email address *

Please enter your email address

Enter your email

Make sure the files are formatted properly *

Add additional information

Submit

Figure 5.76

Figure 5.77 shows the upload box with three files ready to go and the other fields filled out. Once everything looks good, they can click on the *Submit* button to have their files uploaded to my account.

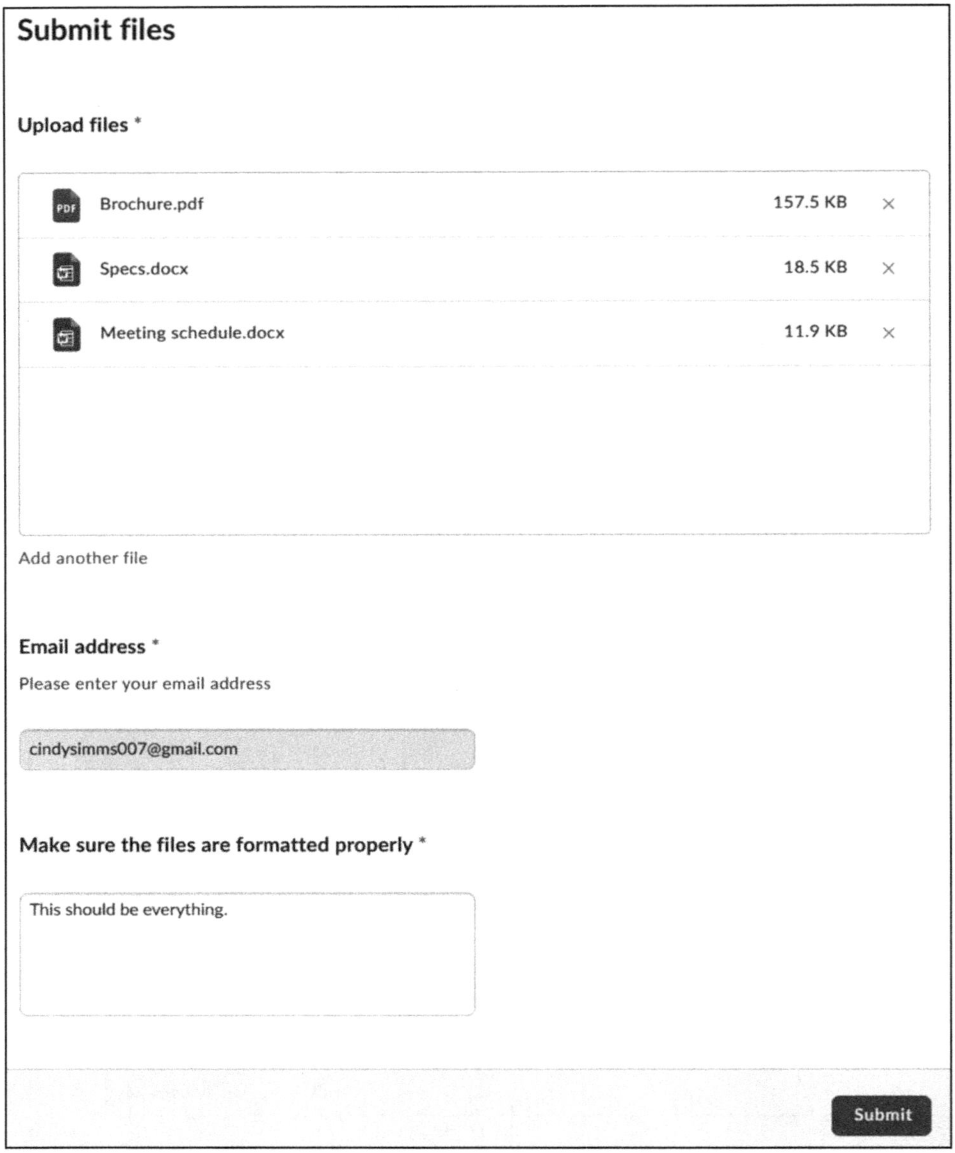

Submit files

Upload files *

PDF Brochure.pdf	157.5 KB	×
Specs.docx	18.5 KB	×
Meeting schedule.docx	11.9 KB	×

Add another file

Email address *
Please enter your email address

cindysimms007@gmail.com

Make sure the files are formatted properly *

This should be everything.

Submit

Figure 5.77

When I go to my Construction Project Files folder, I will see the three files that they have uploaded to my account.

All Files > **Construction Project Files**

NAME	UPDATED ↑	SIZE
Calendar.docx	Today by Todd Simms	109.8 KB
Brochure.pdf	(i) Today by cindysimms007...	157.5 KB
Meeting schedule.docx	(i) Today by cindysimms007...	11.9 KB
Specs.docx	(i) Today by cindysimms007...	18.5 KB

Figure 5.78

If I go to the Admin Console and then the *File Requests* section, I will see this file request and any others I have set up in the past. I can then click on the ellipses to deactivate or delete the file request link.

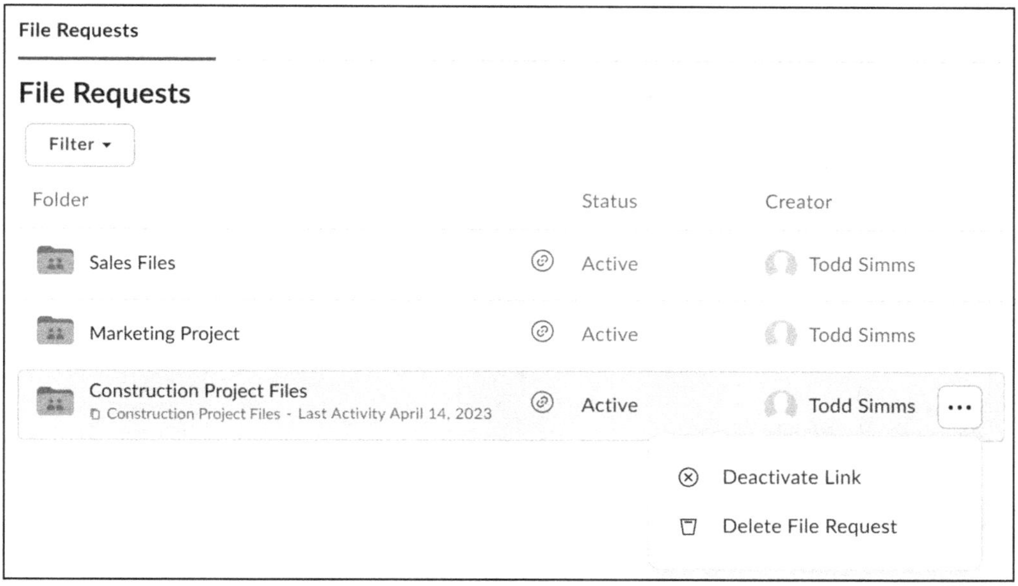

File Requests

File Requests

Filter ▾

Folder	Status	Creator	
Sales Files	Active	Todd Simms	
Marketing Project	Active	Todd Simms	
Construction Project Files Construction Project Files - Last Activity April 14, 2023	Active	Todd Simms	...

⊗ Deactivate Link

🗑 Delete File Request

Figure 5.79

Box Mobile App

If you require access to your files no matter where you happen to be, you can install the Box mobile app on your smartphone or tablet so you can always have your files ready to work on at a moment's notice.

The Box app is available for Apple (iPhone) and Android devices, and it is installed just like any other app you might have added to your device. When you search for Box, just be sure to install the correct app and look for the Box logo as seen in figure 5.80. The developer's name should also say Box as well.

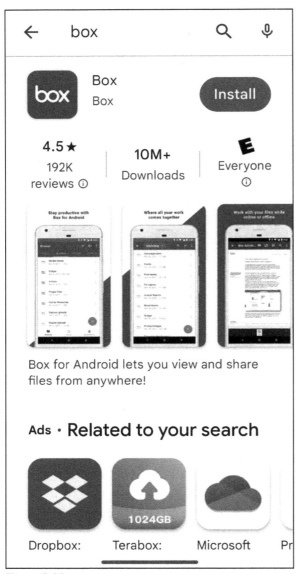

Figure 5.80

Once you install the app and log in, you will then see your files and folders just like you do on your PC. You will have the typical All Files section as well as recent files just like you do on the Box website.

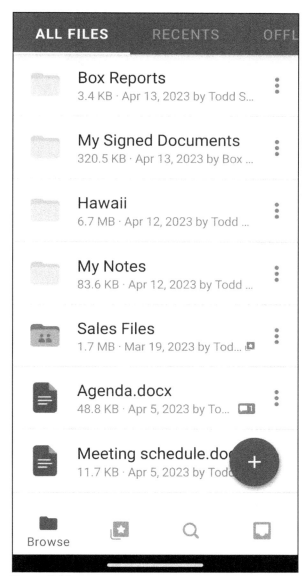

Figure 5.81

If you tap on the + icon, you will then be able to do things such as create a new folder or new document as well as upload files from your device. You can also use the *Capture Media* option to take a photo or video as well as scan a document or record audio. Then this media will be uploaded to your Box account so you can use or share it with others. There is also the option to create a new Box Note just like you can on your computer.

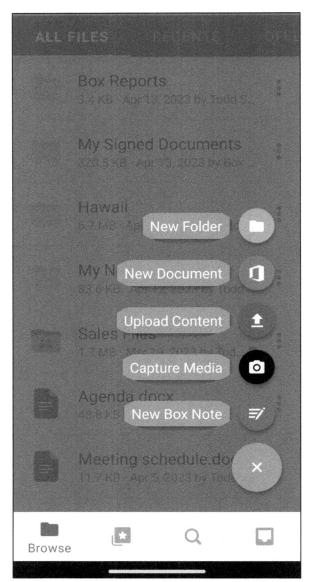

Figure 5.82

The *Offline* section can be used to access files when you do not have an active internet connection. This is rare for smartphones but can come in handy for tablet users who still need to access certain files offline. To make a file available offline, simply tap on the three vertical dots next to it and choose the *Make available offline* option as seen in figure 5.84.

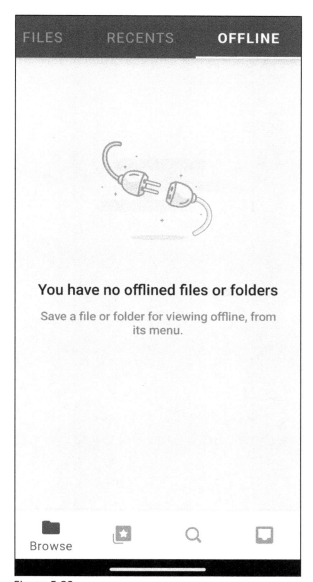

Figure 5.83

When you tap on the three vertical dots next to a file, you will have several other options such as the ability to share, download, copy, move, rename and delete the file. And of course, you can open the file just by tapping on the file name itself.

179

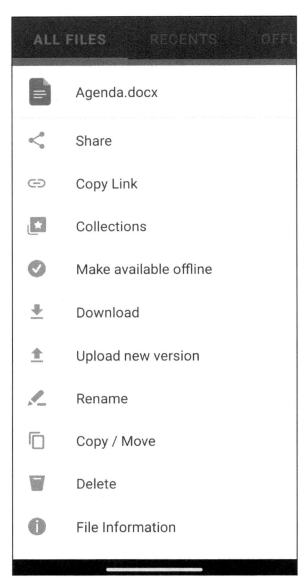

Figure 5.84

Tapping on the three vertical dots next to a folder name will give you similar options to what you saw when doing the same thing with your files.

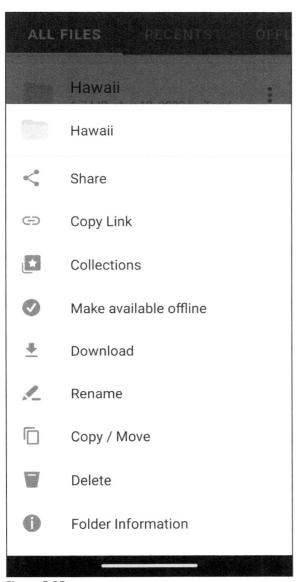

Figure 5.85

At the bottom of the app, you will also have a section that you can use to view your favorites and collections.

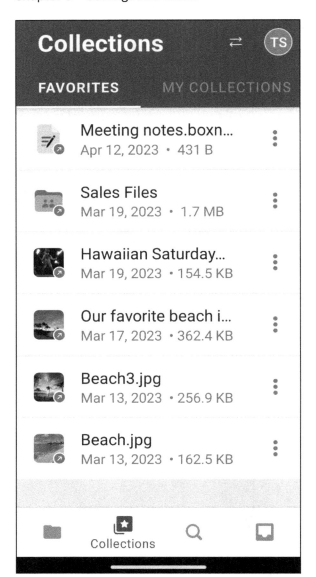

Figure 5.86

Tapping on your profile letters or image will take you to the Box app settings where you can view information about your account, log out, change notification settings, change security settings and get help.

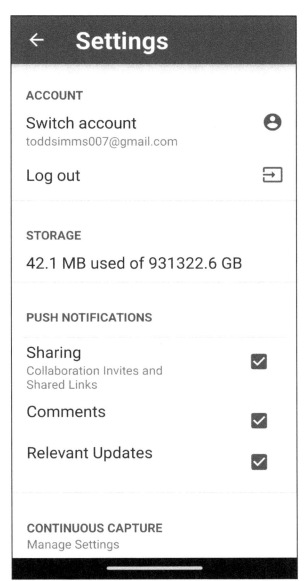

Figure 5.87

What's Next?

Now that you have read through this book and taken your Box skills to the next level, you might be wondering what you should do next. Well, that depends on where you want to go. Are you happy with what you have learned, or do you want to further your knowledge or try out some of the more advanced features that come with the Personal, Business or Enterprise plans?

If you do want to expand your knowledge on other cloud technology-related topics, you should look at subject-specific books such as cloud storage or hosted servers and services. Focus on one subject at a time, then apply what you have learned to the next subject. You can also check my other books that cover a wider range of topics mentioned above and then some.

There are many great video resources as well, such as Pluralsight or CBT Nuggets, which offer online subscriptions to training videos of every type imaginable. YouTube is also a great source for training videos if you know what to search for.

If you are content with being a Box power user that knows more than your friends, then just keep on reading up on the technologies you want to learn, and you will soon become your friends and family's go-to computer person, which may or may not be something you want!

Thanks for reading **Box Made Easy**. You can also check out the other books in the Made Easy series for additional computer-related information and training. You can get more information on my other books on my Computers Made Easy Book Series website.

https://www.madeeasybookseries.com

COMPUTERS MADE EASY	WINDOWS 10 MADE EASY	NETWORKING MADE EASY	CLOUD STORAGE MADE EASY	GOOGLE APPS MADE EASY
OFFICE MADE EASY	android SMARTPHONES MADE EASY	THE INTERNET MADE EASY	WINDOWS HOME NETWORKING	BUILDING YOUR OWN COMPUTER
PHOTOSHOP ELEMENTS	POWERPOINT MADE EASY	PUBLISHER MADE EASY	PREMIERE ELEMENTS	VIRTUALBOX MADE EASY
ZOOM MADE EASY	GOOGLE MEET MADE EASY	SLACK MADE EASY	GOOGLE CLASSROOM	GOOGLE DOCS
GOOGLE SITES	OFFICE FOR THE WEB	WIX MADE EASY	WINDOWS VIDEO EDITOR	COMPUTERS FOR SENIORS
GMAIL MADE EASY	WINDOWS 11 FILE MANAGEMENT	WINDOWS 11 MADE EASY	SOCIAL MEDIA FOR SENIORS	EMAIL FOR SENIORS
DROPBOX MADE EASY	WINDOWS 11 FOR SENIORS	ONENOTE MADE EASY	ANDROID SMARTPHONES FOR SENIORS	WINDOWS MAIL & CALENDAR
GOOGLE DRIVE MADE EASY	THE INTERNET FOR SENIORS MADE EASY	GOOGLE PHOTOS MADE EASY	VMWARE WORKSTATION MADE EASY	CLIPCHAMP VIDEO EDITOR MADE EASY
JAMES BERNSTEIN	JAMES BERNSTEIN	JAMES BERNSTEIN	JAMES BERNSTEIN	JAMES BERNSTEIN

You should also check out my computer tips website, as well as follow it on Facebook to find more information on all kinds of computer topics.

www.onlinecomputertips.com
https://www.facebook.com/OnlineComputerTips/

About the Author

James Bernstein has been working with various companies in the IT field for over 20 years, managing technologies such as SAN and NAS storage, VMware, backups, Windows Servers, Active Directory, DNS, DHCP, Networking, Microsoft Office, Exchange, and more.

He has obtained certifications from Microsoft, VMware, CompTIA, ShoreTel, and SNIA, and continues to strive to learn new technologies to further his knowledge on a variety of subjects.

He is also the founder of the website onlinecomputertips.com, which offers its readers valuable information on topics such as Windows, networking, hardware, software, and troubleshooting. Jim writes much of the content himself and adds new content on a regular basis. The site was started in 2005 and is still going strong today.

www.ingramcontent.com/pod-product-compliance
Lightning Source LLC
LaVergne TN
LVHW081342050326
832903LV00024B/1275